Limitless
MIND

OTHER BOOKS BY RUSSELL TARG

The Heart of the Mind:
How to Experience God without Belief (1999; with Jane Katra)

Miracles of Mind:
Exploring Nonlocal Consciousness and Spiritual Healing
(1998; with Jane Katra)

The Mind Race:
Understanding and Using Psychic Abilities
(1984; with Keith Harary)

Mind at Large: Institute of Electrical and Electronics Engineers
Symposium on the Nature of Extrasensory Perception
(1979, 2002; with Charles Tart and Harold Puthoff)

Mind Reach:
Scientists Look at Psychic Ability (1977; with Harold Puthoff)

Limitless
MIND

a guide to remote viewing and
transformation of consciousness

RUSSELL TARG

New World Library
Novato, California
www.newworldlibrary.com

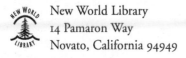

New World Library
14 Pamaron Way
Novato, California 94949

The cartoons on pages 58 and 99 are reprinted by permission of the *New Yorker.* All rights reserved.

Copyright © 2004 by Russell Targ

All rights reserved. This book may not be reproduced in whole or in part, stored in a retrieval system, or transmitted in any form or by any means electronic, mechanical, or other without written permission from the publisher, except by a reviewer, who may quote brief passages in a review.

Front cover design by Cathey Flickinger
Text design and typography by Tona Pearce Myers

Library of Congress Cataloging-in-Publication Data
Targ, Russell.
  Limitless mind : a guide to remote viewing and transformation of consciousness / Russell Targ.
        p.   cm.
Includes bibliographical references and index.
  ISBN 978-1-57731-413-4 (pbk. : alk. paper)
  1. Remote viewing (Parapsychology) 2. Extrasensory perception.
I. Title.
  BF1389.R45T37 2004
  133.8—dc22   2003021766

First Printing, January 2004
ISBN 978-1-57731-413-4
Printed in Canada on 100% postconsumer waste recycled paper.

20 19 18

This book is dedicated
to the memory of my beloved daughter
Dr. Elisabeth Targ,
visionary psychiatrist and gifted healer,
and with limitless love
to my teacher Gangaji.

CONTENTS

ACKNOWLEDGMENTS

I wish to give my profound thanks to my friend and teacher, Dr. H. Dean Brown. A spirit such as Dean's, which has now gained independence from all bondage and achieved absolute consciousness, resides in the realm of *ritam bhara pragyam*. Dean often described this as "the plane of the absolute." This Sanskrit phrase refers to the level of consciousness that knows only truth: the part of us that is unaffected by our daily experiences and is the home of our soul; the clearest, most direct source for answers on our journey.

Dean, who was a distinguished physicist, a mystic, and a Sanskrit scholar, taught that emptiness (*sunyata*) is where we encounter this plane of experience, the domain of eternal form. This is a Vedic concept that corresponds to Plato's field of ideals, Jung's archetypes, and De Chardin's noosphere. The pinnacle of Vedic thought is the idea that our innermost self (*Atman* — ever more subtle, ever contracting) is identical to the entire universe (*Brahman* — ever expanding, cosmic). We are one with everything.

For the thirty years when I knew him, Dean taught that when we approach the universe — play with it, understand it, and produce effects through our pure center — life becomes active and joyful. If we are simply centered, we become nothing and everything. Erwin Schrödinger, who perfected quantum mechanics and was revered by Dean, believed this equating of Atman and Brahman to be "the grandest of all thoughts."

I also wish to sincerely thank Dr. Jane Katra, with whom I wrote two previous books, for stimulating many of the ideas in this book as well. And I thank Dr. Elizabeth Rauscher for her insightful contributions to the chapters that discuss the end of physics and the physics of psychic abilities.

*I consider science an integrating part of our endeavor to answer the
one great philosophical question which embraces all others — who
are we? And more than that: I consider this not only one of the tasks,
but the task, of science, the only one that really counts.*

— Erwin Schrödinger
Science and Humanism

I have been investigating and writing about remote viewing and
extrasensory perception (ESP) for more than thirty years. In
this book, I will try to answer the critical question, "Why bother
with ESP?"

In an author's preface, the reader often has an opportunity to
find out who the author is and what is on his mind. My mind is
presently filled with a mixture of anger, grief, and sadness at the
recent and untimely death of my dear daughter Elisabeth, who left
us in July of 2002 at the age of forty. She was an openhearted psychiatrist, a courageous researcher, a linguist, and a healer who
often worked with me. Although she was a practicing Buddhist
with a Jewish upbringing, from her sickbed she expressed the
desire to be "the Virgin Mary's assistant" — very much in line with
her research in distant healing and distant prayer. I have included
more about Elisabeth's research and our father-daughter ESP
experiments and adventures in the Afterword.

Elisabeth was an inspiration to many people within and
beyond the medical research community. She also brightened my
life and inspired me to write this book. I would not have been

introduced to the possibilities of limitless mind if Elisabeth and
her husband, physicist Mark Comings, had not been so passionate about the *Dzogchen* (great perfection) teachings of the twelfth-
century Buddhist master Longchenpa.[1] In his books I experienced
the magic of trading the fear and suffering of our contemporary
conditioned awareness for the peace and freedom of timeless existence. As the visionary philosopher Gurdjieff describes our condition, we are each like "a machine controlled by accidental shocks
from outside." This is what we must overcome.

As a scientist, I am comfortable saying that Dzogchen teaches
us to look directly at our awareness and experience the geometry
of consciousness — the relationship of our awareness to the space-
time in which we live. Properly understood, these teachings of
expanded awareness and the experience of spaciousness are not
about self-improvement or gaining power; they are about self-
realization: discovering who we really are. Such teaching predates
by more than eight centuries my own efforts for the past decade
to show people how to develop their psychic abilities. To my
mind, the self or ego is not who we are. This can be revealed in
many ways, one of them being the practice of remote viewing.
Among other things, we discover through this process that we are
the flow of loving awareness that is available to us whenever we
are quiet and peaceful. This is the underlying theme of *Limitless
Mind*.

I believe that, in this plane of illusion, we give life all the
meaning it has for us. We give meaning to everything we experience based on our lifelong conditioning. As it is articulated in *The
Tibetan Book of the Dead*,[2] "As a thing is viewed, so it appears." It
appears to me that we are, first and foremost, looking for the experience of love. In a meditative state of mind, we can become aware
that we are not a body, but rather *limitless, nonlocal awareness*
animating or residing as a body. Resting in the spacious flow of

loving awareness — which some call God — we discover that we already have, right now within us, everything we could possibly be looking for. This is what the Hindus call *ananda,* and what Jesus called "the peace that passeth understanding." Our needs and wants are the illusions. The spiritual path called *A Course in Miracles* teaches: "I am not a body. I am free...as God created me."[3] In *Limitless Mind,* I will demonstrate that this is a testable hypothesis that does not require belief in anything.

The data from remote viewing research show, without a doubt, that our mind is limitless and that our awareness both fills and transcends our ordinary understanding of space and time. Psychic abilities, and remote viewing in particular, point to the possibility of our residing in — and as — this state of expanded, timeless, fearless, spacious awareness. Psychic abilities are neither sacred nor secular; they are just natural human abilities. We can use them to find lost car keys or elusive parking spaces, to forecast changes in the stock market, or to discover who we really are. I believe that 99 percent of the value of psychic abilities resides in the opportunity they offer for self-inquiry and self-realization. Let's see if we can accomplish this together.

Russell Targ

Palo Alto, California

August 4, 2002

(Elisabeth Targ's forty-first birthday)

In this small book is compressed a world of ideas — a formula for new ways of being. Within a sturdy background of scientific research and years of conclusive studies, it presents a perspective on our humanity that, until now, would have seemed more mythic than real.

Many have long suspected that the very concepts of "near" and "far" may be a stratagem of our local minds — more a habit or a cultural dictum than the way things really are. But now we discover what poets and mystics have always suspected: Our minds are star-gates, our bodies celled of mysteries; what was taken to be remote is actually our near neighbor in the all-reaching compass of the mind.

Russell Targ has spent a lifetime working in the science of consciousness and human possibilities. His research methods are both rigorous and resourceful, as they must be in such pioneering fields. And yet, in elegant and lucid prose, he shows us the other side of the moon of ourselves. The descriptions of the remote-viewing work that he and his associates have done are both compelling and central to our understanding of the human capacity.

Russell Targ gives us insight into why we sometimes receive information — about a place, an object, a person — that is neither available through normal, local, sensory mechanisms nor explained by classical space-time theories. Where does this apparently intuitive information come from? Why is it that we sometimes gain knowledge with a rapidity that is more like remembering than like any learning process? In exploring these questions, Dr. Targ is one of the new group of brilliant and courageous scientists who are changing our views of the nature of reality.

In this company, we would include the English biologist Rupert Sheldrake and his theory of "morphic resonance." Sheldrake states the very basis of paradigm shift: things are as they are because they were as they were. The laws of nature are not absolutes; rather, they are accumulations of habits. The law of gravity, for example, is a pretty well-fixed habit, probably owing to the trillions of beings throughout the universe who give it general assent. Yet yogis, swamis, and more than a few Catholic saints report that, in deep meditation or spiritual rapture, they have been known to bump their heads on the ceiling. Rapture is nothing if not a paradigm shift.

Laws change, habits dissolve, new forms and functions emerge whenever an individual or a society learns a new behavior. This is because we are all connected through what Sheldrake calls "morphogenetic fields" — organizing templates that weave through time and space and hold the patterns for all structures, but which can be altered according to our changing thoughts and actions. Thus the more an event, skill, or pattern of behavior occurs, the more powerful its morphogenetic field becomes. We know, for example, that people in the twentieth century learned to ride bicycles and use machines more quickly and effectively than did people in the nineteenth century. Similarly, today's children and adolescents learn to use computers in ways that seem beyond the competence of their parents — or, as an adult friend once said when he couldn't get a computer program to work, "Let's call in an expert. Get the kid next door."

Children, some autistic people, idiots savants, people in life-threatening situations, animals who know just when their masters have gotten on the bus to come home — all are participating in this phenomenon. But what is behind it? Recent cutting-edge, state-of-the-art physics now says that it comes from the quantum hologram. In each case I've mentioned, the individuals have gone beyond the bandwidth of local perception and memory and entered a field of knowing in which much larger information can be accessed via the quantum hologram. It has been suggested that this quantum hologram is made of a higher light vibration and holds all knowledge and information. It may be that the lower light vibration — the one that falls within the electromagnetic spectrum and therefore guides our perception — decodes the higher vibration of the quantum hologram.

If we look at how holograms are created on film, we may be able to understand by analogy how this decoding operates. To create a hologram, light from a laser goes through a maze of mirrors and beam-splitters to form two beams of light. A beam-splitter is a half-silvered mirror that allows part of the light (the reference beam) to pass through directly to the film while reflecting part of the light (the illuminating beam) toward the object being pictured, from which it is reflected onto the same film. When the two beams meet, the result of the interference patterns between them is recorded on the film. Where the beams coincide, or are "in phase," there will be enough light to expose the film because the light energy is reinforced at the points of interference. Where the beams are out of phase, they will cancel out each other's energy and leave a dark place on the film. The picture of the object in this resulting film hologram can be seen when laser, or coherent, light decodes it and gives us the picture.

Now amplify this to a universal scale and think of the film as the nonlocal simultaneous-everywhere-and-everything matrix — the quantum hologram itself. It is not a film but a great field of being — the order of the metaverse. Alfred North Whitehead, in 1929, described this field as the great expanding nexus of occurrences beyond sense perception, with all minds and all things inter-locking. More recently, physicist David Bohm referred to it as the primary order of the universe, which is implicate, enfolded, har-boring our reality in much the same way as the DNA in the nucleus of a cell harbors potential life and directs its unfolding.

So the quantum hologram is an order of pure beingness, pure frequency — perhaps the essential Light itself — which tran-scends all specifications and knows neither "here" nor "there." It is the place from which patterns and archetypes arise. It is the realm of love and organicity, the lure of evolution, and the Mind that is minding. It is the realm from which the forms of reality are engen-dered, pervading everything, and potentially totally available at any particular part of our reality.

The secondary order is the decoded hologramatic image of reality, or what Bohm calls "second-generation reality." All appar-ent movement and substance, then, are of this secondary order — that which is explicate, unfolded, manifest in space and time, filled with kittens and quasars and the need to connect with others. Thus, the greater part of our awareness is caught up in Bohm's second-generation reality, while the eternal part of our consciousness is forever contained in the primary, implicate order, or quantum hologram. We all have it in us to travel back and forth between the two orders, for our brains seem to serve both as gates into God and as hologramatic reducing valves that render God-stuff into structure and form.

This is where Russell Targ's work becomes relevant to all of us. It is about training human reality to be very fluid, moving back and forth between ordinary and extraordinary realities, local and archetypal worlds, implicate and explicate domains.

Most, if not all, of the subtle, ephemeral, and unexplained phenomena associated with subjective experience are probably connected, directly or indirectly, with the nonlocal nature of the quantum hologram. These phenomena run the gamut from telepathy to mystical experience. In this regard, what we call "psychic phenomena" are only by-products of this simultaneous-everywhere matrix. And synchronicity — those coincidental occurrences that seem to reflect some higher design or connected-ness — would seem to derive from the purposeful, patterning nature of the primary order, wherein everything is interconnected regardless of how distant in space or time. In fact, there is no such thing as coincidence in the usual sense, for everything is co-inciding; thus the remarkable results that Targ and his team have been able to elicit. What this book demonstrates is that the phe-nomena that have hitherto seemed extraordinary are really just a fascinating subset of reality in general. The brain, then, can be described in part as a quantum computer. Consciousness emerges from quantum processes in the brain — that is, from the inter-reaction between your perception on the electromagnetic spec-trum and the quantum, more ultimate spectrum of light. Targ's research not only implies what quantum physics affirms — the fundamental transformation of the scientific worldview — it also demonstrates the quantum aspects inherent in our human nature. This has tremendous implications for philosophy, psychology, and metaphysics.

Think of local consciousness on the electromagnetic spectrum of light as the foreground and quantum mind as the background. Since it is rare that most of us attend to the background, or non-local, during the course of our everyday affairs, we perceive things without the subtle awareness that would bring the full grandeur of reality into play. And yet, as Targ shows so effectively, we all have these capacities for enlarged perception, although they have been stunted by habit, conditioning, and the cultural trance. With the kinds of training offered by Targ and other disciplines related to non-ordinary states of consciousness, it is possible that many individuals can learn to use their mind-brain systems in ways that open the doors of their perceptions to receive the news from the universe. It is likely that Einstein and others who testified to making huge creative leaps, then spending years finding the steps that would lead to their conclusions, were actually accessing quantum information rather than extrapolating from factual data.

Given our quantum hologram essence, our minds may well be omni-dimensional. I believe that consciousness has the innate capacity to tune into and modulate with different domains. This implies that we have, within these resonant quantum fields of consciousness, access to different universes. Does this also mean that the mind has the ability to travel in time, to visit ancient Palestine when Christ delivered the Sermon on the Mount, to be present in consciousness at the signing of the Declaration of Independence? Is the past still present, nested in the many frequencies that make up the quantum mind of the Maker?

What seems to be true is that, by changing consciousness, we can experience more profound patterns of the universe. I find, for example, that when we alter awareness toward more meditative or spiritual states, we become citizens of a larger universe in regard to perception, time, space, dimensionality, and possibility; we operate at higher frequencies within the electromagnetic spectrum of the light domain. This is because we are operating from the higher patterns themselves — what I am calling the archetypal domain. It is then, too, that our psychological makeup is less traumatized by past experience, is more capacious and capricious, and we feel extended into a multidimensional universe.

Thus, among many other things, we are able to cause action at a distance. There have been millennia of observations of such phenomena. If prayer had not produced some positive results, religion would have been abandoned centuries ago. Ascribing such results to a supernatural agency rather than to nonlocality simply represents a different mode of description. Look at all the work that has been done in recent years to document the efficacy of prayer, particularly healing prayer. The results in most cases are very suggestive of nonlocal effects.

Limitless Mind invites the reader to dwell in possibility. Russell Targ and his associates, especially his beloved daughter Elisabeth, bring certainty to what until recently was considered merely anecdotal. In so doing, they give us a universe that is larger than our aspirations and richer than all our dreams. For this we are very grateful.

Jean Houston

the unknowable
end of science

Most people have the ability to describe and experience events and locations that are blocked from ordinary perception. *Limitless Mind* illustrates this perceptual ability by presenting decades of experiments in *remote viewing,* or remote perception of events. Such abilities have been demonstrated and documented in numerous U.S. and international laboratories, including the laboratory of Stanford Research Institute (SRI) in California, where a program of investigation began thirty years ago. However, despite repeated corroboration of our natural capacity for such psychic abilities, mainstream science has not accepted these abilities as real. How can this be?

As one of the scientists who conducted the research at SRI, I do not have to believe in ESP. For decades, I have seen ESP occur in the laboratory on a day-to-day basis. As a physicist, I don't have to believe in this phenomenon any more than I have to believe in the existence of lasers — with which I have also worked extensively. Psychic abilities exist, just as lasers do, as has been repeatedly demonstrated by hundreds of experimental research studies. What I believe in is good scientific data and replicated experiments, and those are what I describe in this book.

There is a skeptical community that works tirelessly to "save" science from the depredations of frauds and charlatans. I applaud them, and I think they play a valuable role. In science, however, it is just as serious an error to ignore real but unpredictable data as it is to accept false data as true. For example, neglecting a small, fluctuating signal from an air turbulence detector can cause an airplane to crash — something that has actually happened.

Naturally, none of us want to appear gullible, silly, or insane. We would often prefer to be wrong with the support of a group than to be correct all by ourselves. Offering scientific opinions contrary to the prevailing paradigm puts one in a similar position to such currently respected men as Giordano Bruno and Galileo Galilei, who suffered in their day for offering correct but unpopular scientific opinions about the earth's motion. Commenting on this hazard, Voltaire wrote, "It is dangerous to be right in matters on which the established authorities are wrong."

Similarly, many people today are reluctant to acknowledge the reality of psychic abilities, even though a 2001 Gallup poll stated that more than half the U.S. population reports having had psychic experiences. These believers include two-thirds of the college graduates and university professors queried. Such experiences, however, are strongly repressed in this society. Mainstream scientists usually declare them to be without credibility, and many organized religions declare them to be bad, or even evil.

For millennia, philosophers have invited us to discover who we really are and what abilities we actually have, but we often feel afraid to do so because such exploration can be dangerous. In the sixteenth and seventeenth centuries, Copernicus, Bruno, and Galileo were persecuted because they showed overwhelming evidence that we were not, in fact, special beings at the center of the universe, as everyone had been taught. Instead, we were (and are) inhabitants of one of several large rocks a hundred million miles from the sun, at the edge of the galaxy. People have always hated this idea. It was an attack on their egos — on who they thought they were. In the nineteenth century, when Charles Darwin demonstrated that we are also first cousins to monkeys and chimpanzees, it was a further assault on our pride!

Another blow to our egos came not much later, when Sigmund Freud showed that much of what we believe and experience is governed by our subconscious, of which we are entirely unaware. The experience of psychic abilities further erodes the boundaries of the self by indicating that the psychic shell separating us from each other is really quite porous. -

In actuality, modern physics shows that our consciousness connects us quite intimately. Nobel physicist Erwin Schrödinger described our profound interconnectedness this way:

> Consciousness is a singular of which the plural is unknown. There is only one thing, and that which seems to be a plurality is merely a series of different aspects of this one thing, produced by a deception, the Indian *maya*, as in a gallery of mirrors.[1]

Such realizations of one consciousness can give rise to a fear of uncontrolled, telepathic intimacy, and a possibly troubling loss of privacy. As our personal egos are diminished by advances in scientific knowledge, however, our concept of who we are is greatly enhanced. As we learn to surrender more and more of our attachment to our egos, we can participate in the most profound

intimacy without fear of losing ourselves. We can share the energetic flow of loving awareness with others and expand our knowledge of who we really are. Intimacy is not to be feared; it is to be
celebrated. What we discover from the data of "psi," or psychical
research, is that we are capable of expanded awareness far beyond
our physical bodies.

In fact, the principle finding of this research demonstrates
that there is no known spatial or temporal limit to our awareness.
That is to say, in consciousness there is only one of us here. Or, as
the Buddhists and quantum physicists continuously remind us,
"Separation is an illusion."

NO END TO SCIENCE IN SIGHT

We often hear that the end of physics is just a few years away —
to be described, as Michio Kaku recently said, "with an equation
less than one inch long."[2] Similarly, Nobel laureate physicist
Steven Weinberg recently published a long essay in the *New York
Review of Books* describing his "search for the fundamental principles that underlie everything."[3] He added, however, that "science
in the future may take a turn that we cannot now imagine. But, I
see not the slightest advance sign of such a change" (my emphasis).

Scientists have been saying this sort of thing for more than a
century. For example, in the late 1800s Lord Kelvin made the now-
famous statement that physics was complete, except that "only
two small clouds remain on the horizon of the knowledge of
physics." The two clouds were: first, the interpretation of the
results of the Michelson-Morley experiment (which did not detect
any effects of the widely hypothesized "aether"), and second, the
failure of then-contemporary electromagnetic theory to predict
spectral distribution of black-body radiation. These little clouds
led to the discovery of special relativity, quantum mechanics, and
what we think of today as modern physics.

In 1975, at Lawrence Berkeley Laboratory, the same Steven Weinberg declared, "What we want to know is the set of simple principles from which the properties of particles, and hence everything else, can be deduced." Then, at Cambridge University in 1980, revered astrophysicist Stephen Hawking told his audience, "I want to discuss the possibility that the goal of theoretical physics might be achieved in the not-too-distant future, say, by the end of the twentieth century. By this I mean that we might have a complete, consistent, and unified theory of physical interactions that would describe all possible observations." Not only did this not happen, but I posit that it is unlikely to happen. As I write this, physicists are still struggling to explain newly discovered dark matter, dark energy, and the very surprising accelerating expansion of the universe (or, is it a change in the supposedly constant velocity of light?).

To my mind, the most shocking example of a brilliant man saying something truly silly is a quote from A. A. Michelson, after he showed that there was no aether, but before the discovery of relativity and quantum mechanics. Expressing the spirit of his time, he said, "The most important fundamental laws and facts of physical science have all been discovered, and these are now so firmly established that the possibility of their ever being supplemented in consequence of new discoveries is exceedingly remote."[4]

I believe that these "end of physics" statements are not only untrue, but misleading and logically impossible. The hubris of brilliant and famous scientists is still with us today. The issue is very important, because it shows what terrible trouble we can get into if we are totally lacking in awe, wonder, or spiritual questioning.

Great visionary scientists such as Einstein, Newton, and John Archibald Wheeler had no such lack. At ninety, Wheeler was still asking, "How come the universe?" In his writing, Einstein said that we "use our intellect to solve difficult problems, but the problems themselves come from another source."

We may well ask: Will there be an end to mathematics? To biology? To history? Will the human mind withdraw from science? Does curiosity ever achieve completion? I think not. A thousand years from now, our current views of physics will seem as primitive as the phlogiston theory seems to us today. (In the eighteenth century, phlogiston was believed to be an element that caused combustion or was given off by anything burning; the notion has long since been discarded.)

Ancient spiritual and philosophical teachings with their roots in India and Tibet assert that consciousness has existed since the beginning of time. However, this consciousness has been unrecognized because of our ignorance of our own true nature. This seemingly radical idea of nonlocal connections is finding increasing acceptance in the data of modern physics, of all places. Thus, it seems appropriate to begin Chapter 1 by discussing the ways in which contemporary physics shows that there are "nonlocal" connections called quantum interconnectedness — that is, an instantaneous spanning of space and time. In Chapter 1, I also relate these data to similar ideas from Buddhism and other ancient mystical teachings, all of which claim that "separation is an illusion."

Remote viewing is an example of nonlocal ability. It has repeatedly allowed people to describe, draw, and experience objects and activities anywhere on the planet, contemporaneously or in the near future.[5] Although we do not yet know how this works, there should no longer be any doubt that most of us are capable of experiencing places and events that appear to be separated from our physical bodies by space and time. In Chapter 2, I present the evidence from remote viewing experiments — my own as well as my colleagues' — showing the reality of these psychic abilities. Then, in Chapter 3, I describe how you can discover these abilities in yourself and incorporate them into your life, including detailed exercises from our remote viewing workshops.

The practice of remote viewing may reveal more to you than simply what's in a paper bag in the other room; it may reveal the nature of your limitless mind — who you really are.

I explore precognition in Chapter 4, including what I consider to be the most important scientific fact from psychical research: It is no more difficult to describe an event that is to occur in the future than to describe an event occurring at the present moment — casting into doubt our understanding of causality itself.

Chapter 5 describes the data and techniques that people use to intuitively diagnose illness. Psychic diagnosis goes beyond the doctor who can make a correct "snap" decision as soon as she sees the patient; here we describe the ability to diagnose illnesses without ever seeing the patient! In Chapter 6, I present the most recent research data on the efficacy of distant prayer and distant healing (categorized as "Distant Mental Influence of Living Systems," or DMILS). Whereas Chapters 2, 3, 4, and 5 deal with the inflow of information from the world, Chapter 6 examines the outflow of healing intention.

Finally, in Chapter 7 I talk about the relationship between remote viewing and spirituality, and how such understanding can fill us with love and free us from fear. I describe the practice of self-inquiry as a way to move beyond our thoughts, out of conditioned awareness, and into a more spacious, peaceful way of life. I have often said that in my past work I was a psychic spy for the CIA and found God — just one of those so-called unintended consequences. (Our program at SRI provided valuable information to almost every branch of the U.S. intelligence community during the Cold War with the Soviet Union.) In this last chapter, I share my experience of how this research led me to philosophical and spiritual teachings that have transformed my consciousness and changed my life in unexpected and rewarding ways.

Limitless
MIND

our limitless

mind

LIVING IN A NONLOCAL UNIVERSE

To see a World in a Grain of Sand
And a Heaven in a Wild Flower,
Hold Infinity in the palm of your hand
And eternity in an hour.

— William Blake

All of life begins on the edge. The first cellular membranes began at the ocean's edge, drying out and being covered with foam, cooling and warming. The edge is a place of opportunity, whether it be a seacoast or an airport. In remote viewing experiments, we find that edges — where land meets water, for instance — are among the easiest locations to see psychically.

The edge further represents a place of change and spaciousness. Port cities at the water's edge have always been a source of

information, excitement, and new possibilities. I am grateful to
live near beautiful San Francisco, on the far edge of the continent.
The mystic, however, knows that he or she is always on the edge
(or any other place of his or her choosing) — in consciousness. It
doesn't matter where one's physical body happens to be; when we
find ourselves truly on the edge, there is an opportunity for an
event, a spiritual teacher, or a friend to pry loose the fingers of lim-
itation one by one and set us free.

In this book, I describe remote viewing in detail — a process
in which you can quiet your mind and *inflow* information from
anywhere in the world. I also discuss distant healing, in which you
can *outflow* your intentions to heal or relieve the pain of a distant
person.

We begin at that still place — on the edge — between the
inflow and the outflow. This is a quiet mental place where nothing at all is happening except the experience of loving awareness in
the present moment, in the now. This archetypal feeling of nonseparation from all of humanity and nature is what Jesus called
"the peace that passeth understanding." Although I have successfully used ESP to spy on the Soviets during the Cold War — even
to forecast changes in the silver commodity market — it is exploring states of peaceful, loving awareness that makes the study of
psychic abilities interesting to me today. As a physicist, I am also
deeply interested in our nonlocal nature.

Sir Arthur Eddington was one of the premier astrophysicists
in the early twentieth century. He wrote extensively about both
the origin of the cosmos and his personal journeys into the peaceful, meditative realms — what he describes as "glimpses of transcendent reality." Sir Arthur writes:

> If I were to try to put into words the essential truth revealed
> by the mystic experience, it would be that our minds are
> not apart from the world; and the feelings that we have of

gladness and melancholy and our other deeper feelings are not of ourselves alone, but are glimpses of reality transcending the narrow limits of our particular consciousness.... [1]

This is a message from a man of limitless mind, who invites us to visit the nonlocal existence beyond space and time.

WHAT WE MEAN BY NONLOCALITY

We live in a "nonlocal" reality, which is to say that we can be affected by events that are distant from our ordinary awareness. This is an alarming idea for an experimental physicist, because it means that laboratory experiments are subject to outside influences that may be beyond the scientist's control or knowledge. In fact, the data from precognition research strongly suggest that an experiment could, in principle, be affected by a signal sent from the future! So a short answer to the question, "How is it that I can psychically describe a distant object?" is that the object is not as distant as it appears. To me, these data suggest that all of space-time is available to your consciousness, right where you are. You are always on the edge.

Nonlocality is a property of both time and space. In a vivid example of nonlocality, studies of identical twins who were separated at birth and reared apart show that the twins share striking similarities in their tastes, interests, spouses, experiences, and professions, beyond what one could reasonably ascribe to their common DNA. One famous set of twins reared far apart were both named Jim by their adoptive parents. Although they never communicated, each twin married a woman named Betty, divorced her, and then married a woman named Linda. They were both firemen, and each had felt a compulsion to build a circular white bench around a tree in his backyard just before coming to their first meeting at the University of Minnesota. I can believe that there might be fireman genes, or music genes, but I don't believe that there are Linda genes, Betty genes, or white bench genes. This looks to me like a nonlocal telepathic connection — inexplicable, but real.[2]

The physics of nonlocality is fundamental to quantum theory. The most exciting research in physics today is the investigation of what physicist David Bohm calls "quantum interconnectedness," or nonlocal correlations. This idea was first proposed in 1935 in a paper by Einstein, Podolsky, and Rosen (EPR) as evidence of a "defect" in quantum theory. In this paper, Einstein called non-local correlation a "ghostly" action at a distance.[3] The seeming paradox of EPR was later formulated as a mathematical proof by J. S. Bell.[4] It has now been repeatedly demonstrated that two quanta of light, given off from a single source and traveling at the speed of light in opposite directions, can maintain their connection to one another. We find that such photons are affected by what happens to their twins, even many miles away. John Clauser (with Stuart Freedman) at the University of California at Berkeley, was the first to demonstrate nonlocality in the laboratory. He recently described to me his impressions of these experiments, saying, "Quantum experiments have been carried out with twin photons, electrons, atoms, and even large atomic structures such as 60-carbon-atom Bucky balls. It may be impossible to keep anything in a box anymore."[5]

Bell further emphasizes: "No theory of reality compatible with quantum theory can require spatially separate events to be independent." That is to say, the measurement of the polarization of one photon determines the polarization of the other photon at its distant measurement site. This surprising coherence between distant entities is called "nonlocality" by Bell, Bohm, Clauser, and others. Physicist Henry Stapp of the University of California at Berkeley states that these quantum connections could be the "most profound discovery in all of science."[6]

Einstein, of course, was correct in saying that there was a correlation between photons receding from each other at the speed of light. It seems, however, that he was mistaken in his concern about the correlation violating relativity theory, because so far it appears that it does not. That is, there is no faster-than-light signaling. EPR analysis from the 1930s, together with contemporary experiments, gives scientific support to the current view of nonlocal connectedness. My colleagues and I do *not* believe, however, that EPR-type correlations are, in themselves, the explanation for mind-to-mind connections, but we do think that they are an unequivocal laboratory example of the nonlocal nature of our universe. And it is this nonlocality that makes these EPR and ESP connections possible.

Data from dream research also provide convincing evidence that our minds have access to events occurring in distant places — and even into the future. The latter was demonstrated by J. W. Dunne's *An Experiment with Time,*[7] in which he recorded, verified, and published his precognitive dreams, as well as by remote-viewing research performed at SRI and Princeton University. The Princeton research showed conclusively that remote viewing exists, with a departure from chance expectation of 10^{-10} (odds of one in ten billion). They found, from 277 formal remote viewing trials, that there is no evidence for a decrease in accuracy or reliability when looking days into the future or thousands of miles into the distance. That is, it is no harder to describe tomorrow's remote viewing target location than it is to describe today's.[8]

Immanuel Kant states that space and time are but modes of human perception, not attributes of the physical world. These modes are powerful filters of our own invention, and they often serve to limit our experience.

I know, based on experimental data from psi research in my laboratory at SRI, that a viewer can focus attention at a specific location anywhere on the planet (or off of it) and often describe what is there. The SRI experiments showed that the viewer is not bound by present time. In contemporary physics, we call this ability to focus attention on distant points in space-time "nonlocal awareness." Data from the past twenty-five years have shown that a remote viewer can answer any question about events anywhere in the past, present, or future, and be correct more than two-thirds of the time. For an experienced viewer, the rate of correct answers can be much higher.

Physicist David Bohm argues that we greatly misunderstand the illusion of separation in space and time. In his textbook, *The Undivided Universe,* he defuses the illusion of separation as he writes about quantum interconnectedness: "The essential features of the implicate order are that the whole universe is in some way enfolded in everything, and that each thing is enfolded in the whole."9

This fundamental statement describes the metaphor of the holographic ordering of the universe. It says that, like a hologram, each region of space-time contains information about every other point in space-time. This information is readily available to our awareness. In the holographic universe of David Bohm, there is a unity of consciousness — a "greater collective mind" — with no boundaries of space or time.

From the current paradigm of modern physics, there is no contradiction between the data of remote viewing and the experienced oneness of consciousness. Nobel-prizewinning physicist Eugene Wigner has written, "The laws of quantum mechanics cannot be formulated without recourse to the concept of consciousness."10

THE PHYSICS OF MIRACLES

The most satisfactory physical description of psi phenomena that I have examined (with theoretical physicist Elizabeth Rauscher) is a nonlocal mathematical model of space-time known as "complex Minkowski space."[11] Herman Minkowski invented the four-dimensional space-time that Einstein used to describe his special relativity. Ordinary Minkowski space consists of three real space dimensions (x, y, z) and one imaginary time dimension (ict), in which "i" is the square root of −1, "c" is the speed of light, and "t" is time. This model is consistent with the foundations of quantum mechanics, Maxwell's formalism for electromagnetism, and the theory of relativity. It is very important that any model constructed to describe psi must not at the same time generate weird or incorrect physics.

The complex Minkowski space is a purely geometrical model formulated in terms of space and time coordinates, in which each of the familiar three spatial (distance) and one temporal (time) coordinates is expanded by two into their real and imaginary parts — making a total of six spatial and two temporal coordinates. There are now three real and three imaginary spatial coordinates, together with the real and imaginary time coordinate.

The *metric* (the standard of how we measure distance and time) of this complex eight-space is a measure of the structure of space-time where we live. Within this structure, we can define the manner in which one physically or psychically moves along a space-time path referred to as a "world line." This movement can be as mundane as meeting a friend tomorrow at 4:00 P.M. on the corner of 42nd Street and Broadway, or as cosmic as experiencing oneness with the universe. Essentially, real-time remote viewing — or any psychic experience — demands that the awareness of the individual is not separate from (or is "contiguous with") a specific target at a distant location. This ability to nonlocally access information that is blocked from ordinary perception can be described as the result of an apparent zero-separation between the viewer and the target. Similarly, in order for precognition to occur, one must be contiguous in awareness with the future event that is sensed. The complex eight-space model can always provide a path (the "world line") in space and time that connects the viewer to a remote target so that the viewer experiences zero spatial and/or temporal distance in the metric.

It appears that, in the realm of consciousness, there may or may not be a separation, depending on one's intention. It is evident to Dr. Rauscher and me that remote-viewing abilities are fundamental to our understanding of consciousness itself. In fact, psi functioning may be the means that consciousness uses to make itself known in the internal and external physical world.

Dr. Rauscher and I recognize that every theory of being is perishable, and that one day it may be found that complex Minkowski space is not the best model for psi. We are confident, however, that two factors will remain: (1) that these phenomena are not a result of an energetic transmission, and (2) that they are, rather, an interaction of our awareness with a nonlocal, hyperdimensional space-time in which we live.

How does consciousness access this nonlocal space? We believe it does so through the process of intentionality, which is fundamental to any goal-oriented process including retrieval of memory. In fact, the universality of nonlocality is simply there, existing as the fundamental nature of space and time. That is, it is not a physical thing, but it is available to be accessed at will.

It now seems clear that ordinary people can access nonlocal space. We have seen remarkable results in hundreds of remote-viewing trials with hundreds of viewers, in the laboratory and in public workshops all over the world. Without a doubt, people can learn to use their intuitive consciousness in a way that transcends conventional understanding of space and time to describe and experience places and events that are blocked from ordinary perception. The whole force of the data in this book shows this to be true.

So the phenomenon exists, but how does it work? We don't know the complete answer to that question, although some things about the answer are known. For example, the data from more than a hundred years of psi research show that there is no significant decline in the accuracy of any kind of ESP with increasing distance between the viewer and the object viewed. We also know that it is no more difficult to look a short distance into the future than it is to describe a present-time hidden target. The data supporting these two assertions, from both SRI and Princeton, are very strong.

We can also conclude from the data that it is very unlikely that any kind of electromagnetic field is involved in carrying psi signals. We conclude this because the very geometry of our three-dimensional space requires that signal strength decrease as you get farther from the source. In fact, an electromagnetic signal decreases in proportion to the square of the distance. That is, the radio signal you receive ten miles from the transmitter is 100 times weaker than the signal you pick up at one mile. At 10,000 miles distance, as in our Moscow-to-San-Francisco experiments, the radio signal would be 100 million times weaker than it would be at one mile away. Yet we do not see the slightest evidence of such a distance-related decrease in psi ability, even though the popular model for ESP involves some kind of mental radio in which my mind "sends a signal" to your mind. We believe that this is probably not a valid model.

In spite of the problem with this model, there is a wonderful book called *Mental Radio*, originally written in 1930 by the great American novelist and muckraker Upton Sinclair.[12] This book contains an extremely valuable description of the psychic process, written by Sinclair's intensely psychic wife Mary Craig. Sinclair and his wife did hundreds of picture-drawing experiments with remarkable success. The book even has a favorable preface by Einstein, who was a friend of the Sinclairs.

Instead of signals being sent, the data suggest that the desired
information is always present and available. In remote viewing, as
well as in healing, the agent's focused intention calls forth the
information. Psychic healers and remote viewers both act as mes-
sengers. In remote viewing, the viewer translates impressions of
the information into drawings and verbal concepts. In psychic
diagnosis, the healer interprets impressions from the patient and
converts them into clairvoyant diagnoses, and sometimes into
energy-manipulating actions to remedy a problem in the patient's
body. Spiritual healing introduces yet another element, whereby
the healer acts as a conduit of healing information to the patient
from the community of spirit in which we all reside, or from God.
Here, the healer makes no translation of the message accessed
from nonlocality, which directly stimulates the patient's cells to
reorganize themselves into a healthy pattern.

To paraphrase the distinguished physicist John Archibald
Wheeler, we would again say that the description of the mechanism of psychic abilities will be found in the geometry of space-
time, and not in the electromagnetic fields. What Wheeler actually
said was, "There is nothing in the world except curved empty
space. Matter, charge, electromagnetism...are only manifesta-
tions of the bending of space. Physics is geometry!"[13] When he
made this assertion in 1957, what Wheeler had in mind was that,
in spite of the successes of quantum theory, the geometrical
approach gives a more comprehensive model of space-time. In
addition, the physical laws that we experience, such as the laws of
gravity and force, derive principally from symmetry laws and from
the geometry of the space-time metric. Symmetry laws describe the
fact that a given physics experiment conducted at different places
or times must give the same result. The law of conservation
of energy, which is the foundation of physics, can be derived

explicitly from these symmetry laws. Similarly, I think that since psi must be compatible with physics, its explanation will also be derived from the geometry of space-time.

When we say that the eventual description of the physics of psi will come from geometry, what we mean is that psi is often seen as paradoxical because we presently misconstrue the nature of the space-time in which we reside. The "naive realist" picture of our reality says that we are each separate creatures sitting on our own well-circumscribed points in space-time. But for the past thirty years, modern physics has been asserting that this model is not correct.

If this explanation does not seem entirely clear, it is probably because, even though Einstein published these ideas sixty years ago, the smartest physicists in the world still do not agree on all of the implications of these nonlocal connections. In fact, Nobel laureate Brian Josephson wrote of quantum physics experiments:

> The existence of such remote influences or connections is suggested more directly by experiments on phenomena such as telepathy (the connection of one mind to another) and psychokinesis (the direct influence of mind on matter), both of which are examples of so-called psi functioning.... One may imagine that life may exist from the beginning as a cooperative whole, directly interconnected at a distance by Bell-type nonlocal interactions, following which modifications through the course of evolution cause organisms to be interconnected directly with each other.... One can see conceptual similarities between psi skills and ordinary skills, e.g. between perceptual skills of hearing and telepathy on the one hand, and between the forms of control of matter involved in control of the body, and in psychokinesis, on the other.[14]

SPIRITUAL AND PHILOSOPHICAL TRADITIONS

In addition to the theories of physicists, the writings of poets and philosophers (some of which originated before biblical times) have articulated the idea that physical separations are more illusory than real. Buddhist teachings, following from the earlier Vedic tradition of 500 B.C., propose that human desires, judgments, and attachments, which arise from distinctions such as "here and not here," "now and not now," are the cause of all the world's suffering.

Aldous Huxley describes the many levels of awareness associated with the "perennial philosophy," a term for the highest common factor present in all the major wisdom traditions and religions of the world.[15] The first principle of Huxley's perennial philosophy is that consciousness is the fundamental building block of the universe; the world is more like a great thought than a great machine. And human beings can access all of the universe through our own consciousness and our nonlocal mind. This philosophy also maintains that we have a dual nature, both local and nonlocal, both material and nonmaterial. Finally, the perennial philosophy teaches that the purpose of life is to become one with the universal, nonlocal, loving consciousness that is available to us. That is, the purpose of life is to become one with God, and then to help others do likewise.

In this worldview, through meditation one experiences increasing unity consciousness as one passes through "the great chain" of physical, biological, mental, spiritual, and etheric levels of awareness. Through meditation, one experiences the insight that one *is* not a body; one *has* a body. Even the idea of "one" is eventually given up in favor of the experience of expanded awareness.

The lesson that separation is an illusion has been spelled out by mystics for at least 2,500 years. Hinduism teaches that individual consciousness *(Atman)* and universal consciousness *(Brahman)* are one. (As I mentioned in the Acknowledgments, physicist

Erwin Schrödinger considered this observation to be the most profound statement in all of metaphysics.)[16] In the Sutras of Patanjali, written 100 years after the Buddha lived, the great Hindu teacher taught that a "realized" being achieves a state of loving awareness in which "the Seer is established in his own essential and fundamental nature (self-realization)." The view of life in which we are all connected with God, and in which the "Kingdom of God" is within us, waiting to be realized and experienced, is part of both the Jewish and Christian traditions — especially in the Thomas gospel.[17] We learn that the loving source we are seeking is immediately available when we make contact with the great "I Am" within each of us.

In Judaism, the local community of spirit is often referred to as *HaShem* (the word), while in Christianity it is called the Holy Spirit, or Emmanuel (the immanent or indwelling God of all). This view of a community of spirit probably arose from mystics of every sacred tradition, whose meditations led them to have oceanic, mind-to-mind feelings of oneness. These realizations may be fleeting or lasting, spontaneous or the product of religious practice, but they are an enduring feature of human life.

When I write about "realizations," I am describing a state in which a practitioner has wisdom of who she or he is, and has embodied that wisdom; it has become integrated into daily life, thoughts, and activities. We often view "awakening" as a first step toward such realization. Awakening can occur in the blink of an eye, frequently through the direct, heart-opening (heart-breaking) transmission of grace from an awakened teacher.

Meditation and working with a spiritual teacher, such as my work with spiritual teacher Gangaji, are two wonderful and proven paths to self-realization. But sublime music, surrendered sexuality, and even certain potentially dangerous drugs such as MDMA (Ecstasy) can stimulate a spiritual awakening together with a transcendent, one-with-God experience of spaciousness.[18] The inspiring and life-affirming tantra teacher Margot Anand describes this opportunity from her tradition. She writes: "Skillful lovers become divine instruments in a symphony of delight. Their communion is ecstasy, the highest state of self-knowing [self-realization] and self-forgetting [spaciousness]." Who would not wish to partake of that?! In my opinion, Margot's heart-opening and humorous approach to love can help us recover from the terrible damage done to the American psyche by our own fundamentalists, the Puritans.

The Tibetan deity Samanthabhadra is a compassionate *bodhisattva* (one who postpones his or her own enlightenment to bring others to enlightenment), whose image is frequently depicted in the inspiring Dzogchen, Buddhist texts of self-liberation. These teachings assume that you are already a peaceful, loving, open-hearted being who is now willing to experience the fast track to spaciousness and timeless awareness. Samanthabhadra is invariably shown in the loving sexual embrace of his partner, Samanthabhadri. Similarly, in quantum physics the material universe is represented by equations called wave functions, a term invented by Erwin Schrödinger, who taught us that in order to manifest as a material object, any entity must appear together with its complex conjugate. In other words, both its real and imaginary parts must be present. That is why these two loving deities are always shown together; in order for either one to manifest, it is necessary to have them both, like the north and south poles of a magnet. That loving exchange of energy is what Margot encourages us to experience on our path to self-discovery.

I once told anthropologist Margaret Mead that I was disappointed about ESP's lack of acceptance in the scientific community. She sternly told me that I shouldn't complain because, after all, Giordano Bruno had been burned at the stake in the sixteenth

Figure 1. Samanthabhadra, the primordial Buddha, and his consort.

century during the Inquisition for espousing ideas not very different from the ones I expressed. Bruno believed in the unity of all
things, and he strongly opposed Aristotelian dualism for separating body and spirit. He exhorted us all to achieve union with the
"Infinite One" in an infinite universe.

Baruch Spinoza, in the seventeenth century, had a similar
worldview; since he was Jewish, he was fortunate to be spared the
Inquisition. He was, however, banished from his own synagogue
because of his pantheistic model of "all things together" comprising God. Einstein said that he "believed in the God of Spinoza,"
which we understand to be the organizing principle of the universe. In the Dzogchen tradition, our personal experience of this
profound principle is known as *dharmakaya,* and it is considered
equivalent to the experience of undifferentiated loving awareness,
or *vajra* (heart-essence). It is the vehicle and the dimension
through which we directly experience the organizing principles of
the universe (the *dharma*).

The philosophy of a universal connection among all things was taught in the 1750s by Bishop George Berkeley, who could be considered an early Transcendentalist. He felt that the world was greatly misapprehended by our ordinary senses, and that consciousness was the fundamental ground of all existence. In the nineteenth century, this idea was expressed by Ralph Waldo Emerson, and today by Christian Science, Science of Mind, and Unity churches.

The coherent theme among all of these is that there is an essential part of all of us that is shared. The famous Swiss psychiatrist Carl Jung described our mind-to-mind connections in terms of a "collective unconscious." Contemporary Judaism teaches a similar view of our interconnectedness. The revered Jewish theologian Rabbi Lawrence Kushner tells us that:

> Human beings are joined to one another and to all creation. Everything performing its intended task doing commerce with its neighbors. Drawing nourishment and sustenance from unimagined other individuals. Coming into being, growing to maturity, procreating. Dying. Often without even the faintest awareness of its indispensable and vital function within the greater "body.". . . All creation is one person, one being, whose cells are connected to one another within a medium called consciousness.[19]

Historically, the belief in our connected nature has largely been based on the personal experiences of the people who promoted the view. Today, we recognize that just because large numbers of people have believed something for several millennia (for example, that the earth is flat), that does not by any means make it true. How are we to decide whether this view of community of spirit is deep nonsense unrelated to nature or a valid concept of the workings of the world? The usual scientific approach is to see if the model offers testable predictions.

The idea that our thoughts transcend space and time is definitely not a new thought. In the collected Buddhist teaching of 500 B.C., recorded in the *Prajnaparamita,* we learn from almost every page that our apparent separation is an illusion and that there is "only one of us here" in consciousness — perhaps not even one.[20] Once this spiritual connection is experienced, compassion for all beings is the natural consequence.

We have the opportunity to experience a self, but that is not who we really are. In fact, in the teaching of the enneagram, a traditional Sufi analysis of character traits and behavior, the self or ego is a fixation from the past; it is conditioned existence — exactly who we are not.[21] The enneagram, brought to us in the 1970s, attempts to make us aware of the extent to which we live in a trancelike attachment to our story of who we think we are. Our "business card," over which we lavish so much attention, is really a kind of "story card" that we give people to tell them who we think we are. If we believe that story, it can cause us a lot of suffering.

In his book on the enneagram, psychologist and spiritual teacher Eli Jackson-Bear makes this important idea poignantly clear. He writes:

> When identification shifts from a particular body...to the totality of being, the soul realizes itself as pure, limitless consciousness. This shift in identification is called Self-realization. In this realization, not only do you find that love is all that there is, *but you also discover that this love is who you are.*[22]

FOUR-VALUED LOGIC

I believe that we are neither a "self" nor "not a self," but that we are awareness residing as a body. This is the sort of apparent paradox about who we are that may not be solvable within the framework of what we call "Aristotelian two-valued logic" — the logic system basic to all of Western analytical thought. In two-valued logic, we frame our reality with questions like "Are we mortal or immortal?" "Is the mind or soul part of the body?" or "Is light made of waves or particles?" But none of these have "yes" or "no" answers. The exclusion of a middle ground between the poles of Aristotelian logic is the source of much confusion. Other logic systems have been suggested in Buddhist writings; the great second-century dharma master and teacher Nagarjuna introduced a four-valued logic system in which statements about the world can be (1) true, (2) not true, (3) both true and not true, and (4) neither true nor not true — which Nagarjuna believed was the usual case—thereby illuminating what is known as the Buddhist Middle Path.[23] According to Nagarjuna, the Buddha first taught that the world is real. He next taught that it is unreal. To the more astute students, he taught that it is both real and not real. And to those who were furthest along the path, he taught that the world is neither real nor not real, which is what we would say today. (In an interview in the magazine *What Is Enlightenment?* the Dalai Lama singled out Nagarjuna as one of the truly enlightened people of all time. He is thought to be a contemporary of Garab Dorjé, the spontaneously awakened discoverer of Dzogchen.)

The two-valued Aristotelian logic we use every day is simply inadequate to describe the data of modern physics, while the four-valued logic system appears quite outside Western consideration and thought. A seeming paradox in physics that may well find its resolution in "four-logic" is the so-called wave/particle paradox. It is well known that, under the conditions of various experimental arrangements, light displays either wave-like or particle-like properties. But what, then, is the essential nature of light? This question may not be amenable to our familiar system of logic, and may be better addressed by an expanded logic system. We might say, for example, that light is (1) a wave, (2) not a wave, (3) both a wave and not a wave, or, most correctly, (4) neither a wave nor not a wave.

This is how we are able to be both a self and not a self — both separated as bodies and not separated in awareness. Four-logic shows that the so-called problem of mind-body duality is not a paradox at all. I discuss this here because four-logic is really the handmaiden of nonlocality, wherein things are neither separate nor not separate.

In the Sutras of Patanjali, which are still in print, the great teacher was not primarily trying to interest people in developing their psychic abilities.[24] He was actually writing a guide on how to become a realized person — how to experience God. He would say that knowing God is part of knowing yourself. The mystic had observed that, once people learn to quiet their minds, they begin to have all sorts of interesting experiences, such as seeing into the distance, experiencing the future, diagnosing illness, healing the sick, and much more. But his goal was to help his students achieve transcendence, rather than to display these *siddhis,* or powers.

I see these abilities, and the mental interconnectedness that they imply, as part of the "perennial philosophy," and I believe they should be seen as matters of experience rather than items of belief. They provide an opportunity to step outside the accepted contemporary paradigm (or religion) of "scientific materialism," in which we are viewed as just being some kind of remarkable sentient meat.

Patanjali also gave step-by-step instructions for what might be called omniscience, as well as the quiet mind. He taught that if one wants to see the moon reflected in a pool of water, one must wait until every ripple is stilled. So it is with mind. He wrote that "yoga (union with God) is mind-wave quieting" and is a first step to either transcendence or knowing God. Achieving omniscience doesn't mean we can know everything. But by asking one question at a time, we can know anything we need to know. It is important to remember that these teachings are not aimed merely at self-improvement; they are designed as a guide to self-realization, or the discovery of who we are. There is a recurring Buddhist caution that "no powers are sought before wisdom" (or liberation from the illusion of who we are). That is, although you may feel that omniscience is coming on, don't get attached to it!

Western spiritual seekers of truth can choose to consciously cultivate what Eastern spiritual traditions describe as mindfulness by developing what can be called "an intimacy with stillness." In Andrew Harvey's book *The Essential Mystics,* he asserts that we may discover that true spirituality is not about passive escape from earthly living but, rather, spirituality is about active arrival here "in full presence." He describes the experience of oceanic love that is available to the quiet mind:

> It always transcends anything that can be said of it, and remains always unstained by any of our human attempts to limit or exploit it. Every mystic of every time and tradition has awakened in wonder and rapture to the signs of this eternal Presence and known its mystery as one of relation and love.[25]

Limitless Mind is an invitation to experience this loving syrup, beyond romance. Although a body can definitely be a vehicle of transformation, love in the Buddhist sense is not about bodies; it is wisdom wedded to compassion. To take the first step toward residing in this state of loving awareness, the Dzogchen master Longchenpa teaches that we must move out of our daily acquiescence to *conditioned awareness* and learn to become aware of, and head in the direction of, *timeless existence.* Conditioned awareness is a distortion of our daily perceptions and experience that is caused by all the "slings and arrows of outrageous fortune" that we have suffered during the entire course of our lives. Almost all spiritual teachings tell us — often to our annoyance — that these experiences are merely illusions. What we are striving for is disillusionment. Conditioned awareness is the crazy-making process of focusing one's anxious and fearful attention on the future, while feeling guilt over the past, and missing out entirely on the present.

A Course in Miracles, which I discuss in the final chapter, explains that by "illusion" we refer to the fact that we subconsciously give all the meaning there is to everything we experience — usually based on something in the past. Things happen, and we then have an opportunity to experience them with naked and unprejudiced awareness, or we can push the events through our filter bank and assign meaning in accordance with today's set of fears, judgments, and agitation.

One of the important repeated teachings of Dzogchen is that *samsara* (everyday material existence in the "rat race") is the same as *nirvana* (the blissful state of surrendered loving awareness). How could this be? My understanding of this paradox is that they are both simply ideas held in the mind. As ideas, one is no more real that the other. Like any idea, fearful or pleasant, it can be released to float away and pop like a soap bubble. Although these teachings were elaborated in the eighth century, they have great currency today, even in the engrams of Freudian psychoanalysis. Engrams are buried memories of traumas, abuse, or indoctrinations that give rise to our subconscious fears, prejudices, and reactions, and which constantly give meaning and color to our experience — without our knowing why.

The spontaneously awakened Dzogchen master Garab Dorjé taught what he knew by direct experience: that our awareness is nonlocal and unlimited by space and time. All of us today can know this truth, based on the data of psychics and parapsychology. But my hope and reason for writing this book is to encourage you to personally investigate the divine opportunity for direct experience of free and timeless awareness.

The reward for embarking on a mind-quieting path is a profound feeling of personal freedom and spaciousness. You will recall that, 2,400 years ago, our friend Patanjali said that quieting the mind is the same as union with God. It still seems to be true today.

on a clear day we
can see forever

WHAT WE KNOW ABOUT REMOTE VIEWING

Remote viewing is not a spiritual path, but such psychic functioning is a step in the direction of conscious awareness — nonlocal mind revealing itself for us to see.

Over time, I have sat in a darkened interview room with hundreds of remote viewers as they shared their mental pictures with me. It is a fact that people can experience a mind-to-mind connection with each other. They can also expand their awareness to describe and experience what is happening in distant locations. Fifty years of published data from all over the world testify to this.

In the fall of 1972, Dr. Hal Puthoff and I started a psychic research program at Stanford Research Institute (SRI). We were both laser physicists who had carried out research for a variety of U.S. government agencies for many years.[1] Our great partner and teacher in the SRI program was the New York artist and highly

respected psychic Ingo Swann. Ingo introduced Hal and me —
and the world — to remote viewing. Actually, the chain of events
went like this: Ingo taught us about remote viewing, we taught the
army, and the army taught the world.[2] The history of our program
is described in several books, including *Miracles of Mind.*[3]

At the time when we began our psi research program, Hal had
already carried out a remarkable experiment with Ingo. In this
trial, Ingo was able to psychically describe and affect the operation
of a highly shielded superconducting magnetometer buried in the
basement of the Stanford University physics building. (This gave
rise to the first of many government inquiries into our activities.)

As a result of this trial, Hal and I began to further investigate
remote viewing, as any physicist would. We put a laser in a box
and we asked Ingo to tell us whether it was on or off. We asked
him to describe pictures that were sealed in opaque envelopes or
hidden in a distant room. He did all these tasks excellently, but he
found them boring. He eventually told us that if we didn't give
him something more interesting to do, he was going back to New
York to resume his life as a painter. He said that if he wanted to
see what was in an envelope, he would open it; to see into the next
room, he would simply open the door. Since he could focus his
attention anywhere in the world (as he told us more than once),
these experiments were a trivialization of his ability! By the end
of the decade, we'd given Ingo many opportunities to psychically
view the world and beyond.

By the beginning of 1974, Hal and I had carried out more
than fifty formal remote viewing trials at SRI, most of which were
low-key experiments with little publicity. However, in 1973 we carried out a series of experiments with the now-famous Israeli psychic Uri Geller that brought us a fair amount of notice. During
the year when we worked with Uri, who demonstrated remarkable
telepathic ability, our tiny program was responsible for more than

half the publicity received by the $100-million SRI. We published
our findings from the work with Uri in the distinguished British
science journal *Nature,*[4] and as a result the SRI psychic research
activity gained worldwide attention.

Figure 2. Russell Targ (left) and Hal Puthoff outside the Stanford Research
Institute, 1977. Photo by Hella Hammid.

Since the beginning of 1973, we also worked with Pat Price, a
retired police commissioner from Burbank, California. Pat had
telephoned Hal and asked if we'd be interested in working with
him. He said that he had used his psychic ability all his life, in particular to catch criminals in his work as a police officer. Of course,
we accepted his offer. Until 1979, when we met Joe McMoneagle,
Pat was the most remarkable psychic we'd ever encountered —
and he remains the only one able to read printed words at a distance. Pat was a cheerful, even-tempered man. A young secretary
who was typing Pat's descriptions of distant sites once asked him
if he could psychically follow her into the ladies' room. His reply

was, "If I can focus my mind on any place on the planet, why would I follow you into the ladies' room?" That was Pat! Figure 3 shows Pat Price on the job.

Figure 3. Retired police commissioner and psychic Pat Price, the only person we know who can psychically read words. Photo by Hella Hammid.

FOUR AREAS OF REMOTE VIEWING APPLICATIONS

Once we learn how to perform remote viewing techniques (which you can do in Chapter 3), how might this process be applied? Dr. Jeffrey Mishlove, in his capacity as Director of the Intuition Network,[5] proposed four broad areas of remote viewing applications: evaluation, location, diagnosis, and forecasting.

Evaluation

Evaluation might include weighing various alternatives, such as an investment or choices of technology or building sites. Evaluation often includes a mixture of psychic ability and nonpsychic intuition. I believe that intuition comprises the sum total of everything one has learned or experienced in the course of one's life and stored in one's subconscious mind; this background then works together with information that comes to one psychically. For example, when I was leaving SRI in 1982, I wondered where I would work next; the employment agency told me that I had destroyed a promising career in lasers by spending ten years doing ESP research. I sat in my office and visualized what my new place of employment would look like. An image of the nearby foothills led me to make inquiries of my friends who worked in the Lockheed Missiles & Space research laboratory. (They were happy to have me return to my laser roots — if I promised not to get them into ESP research.) I believe that a combination of my psychic ability (the information that a job would open up for me at Lockheed) and my intuition (recognition of the foothills and knowing people at Lockheed) helped this image of my possibilities come together.

Location

Remote viewing has been used to find many things of value, including oil or mineral deposits, hidden treasure, and missing people — all of which have been objects of fascination for as long as people have tried to span space with their thoughts. The following story illustrates our experience with this application.

The Kidnapping of Patricia Hearst

On the night of Monday, February 4, 1974, a group of American terrorists kidnapped nineteen-year-old newspaper heiress Patricia Hearst from her apartment near the University of California at Berkeley, where she was a student. The kidnappers identified themselves as the Symbionese Liberation Army (SLA). They were radical anarchists whose slogan was "Death to the fascist insect that preys upon the life of the people." The conservative, wealthy

Hearst family was a perfect target for them. While the press was trying to find "Symbia" on the map, the Berkeley Police Department was trying to locate the daughter of one of the most prominent celebrities in San Francisco — namely the publisher of the *San Francisco Examiner,* and president of the nationwide Hearst newspaper syndicate.

The day after the kidnapping, the police remained clueless. It was such a desperate situation that the Berkeley Police Department was moved to think about asking for psychic guidance. They called the president of SRI on Tuesday afternoon, and our laboratory director asked us if we thought remote viewing could help. Pat Price said that he had often worked on this kind of problem. So we all piled into Hal's car and drove to Berkeley to meet with the detectives on the case and visit the scene of the crime, where pistol shells were still scattered on the floor under the bed.

The kidnappers were known to be violent; two people had been badly beaten, and several neighbors had been shot at during the abduction. It was all quite strange and confusing for Hal and me, but Pat felt very much at home in the Berkeley police station. The detectives had a lot of questions they were planning to ask us. However, Pat stepped forward first and asked the detective who was working with us if he had a "mug book" of local people who were recently out of prison. Yes, they had just such a book. Pat took the book and laid it flat on a wooden table so that we could all see the pages. There were four mug shots on each page. Pat turned the pages after looking carefully at each picture. Then, about ten pages (forty people) into the book, he put his index finger on one of the pictures and said, "He's the leader."

The man Pat singled out from the mug book was Donald "Cinque" DeFreeze, who had managed to escape from California's Soledad Prison a year earlier. Within a week, the detectives were able to verify Pat's remarkable hit.

The police, of course, had no idea where to find DeFreeze. So they asked Pat if he could determine where he might be. Pat sat back in the old oak swivel chair, polished his glasses, and closed his eyes. After a moment of silence, he said, pointing, "They went that way. Is that north?" It was. Pat continued, "I see a white station wagon parked by the side of the road. But they're not in it anymore." The detective asked, "Where can we find the car?" Pat replied, "It's just past a highway overpass, near a restaurant and two large white gas or oil storage tanks." One of the detectives said he knew where that might be. Half an hour later, they found the abandoned car just where Pat said it would be. By that time it was midnight, and Hal and I were happy to go home to more peaceful surroundings. I think Pat could have stayed all night.

After that night, we had several additional opportunities to interact with the Berkeley detectives. As a side note, the most memorable of these for me was a trip to a potential SLA hideout. A detective and I were parked on a tree-covered hillside in the Santa Cruz mountains. The detective asked me if I knew how to handle a gun. I thought this was a surprising request, but I told him that I owned an automatic and knew how to use it. He then handed me his service weapon and said, "Cover my back." He walked around the apparently abandoned house, and I covered him with the gun as he cased the building. I am sure he had no idea that my corrected vision is 20/200, making me legally blind! After that incident, I realized that I was way beyond my psychical-researcher's job description; I retired from the field, feeling that my graduate studies at Columbia had never prepared me for this.

Even during her brutal confinement by the kidnappers, Patricia Hearst had some knowledge of our activities. In her riveting autobiography, she writes:[6]

> Paranoia must be contagious, for everyone in the house had caught it. When Cin [Cinque] came to me one day and

said that the newspapers were reporting that my father had hired psychics to fathom out where I was being kept by the SLA I was paralyzed with fear. "Don't think about any psychics now. Don't communicate with them," he told me. "Focus your mind on something else all the time." I did as I was told. I did not want psychics or anyone else to point the FBI in my direction.

Though Patricia Hearst's concern may seem puzzling, she was wise to be concerned about being killed by her captors if the police showed up at the door.

We continued to work with the Berkeley detectives, and I believe that the kidnappers could have been caught while they were still in Northern California if the Berkeley Police Department, the local sheriff's department, and the FBI had worked together, instead of at cross purposes. (The SLA fiasco seems similar to the noncooperation of the FBI and CIA in the months before 9/11/01 tragedy, when there was essentially no information shared among the agencies. Everyone now agrees that there was plenty of information, but in both cases, it was poorly analyzed.)

The Berkeley Police Department did send a nice letter of commendation to SRI in the end, thanking us for our work on their behalf.

Diagnosis

Diagnosis of medical problems, mechanical problems, safety hazards, sources of human error, and health and environmental hazards are all possible applications for psychic and intuitive practitioners. Medical diagnosis, discussed at length in Chapter 5, is an intriguing example of diagnostic remote viewing. Edgar Cayce, Caroline Myss, and others have demonstrated and refined this practice, which is a much more analytical approach to remote viewing than the other, more intuitive applications we mention in this chapter. For reasons we don't entirely understand, psychic diagnosis is much easier to do than ordinary remote viewing of an object in a box. This may be because it's a more meaningful task, or perhaps the important psychic connection to another living being makes the difference.

I have been practicing remote diagnosis since 2002, and I find it much easier than other forms of remote viewing. Other experienced intuitives have similar experiences. Interestingly, people are beginning to leave me messages asking for diagnostic help.

One such message came from Dr. Jane Katra of Eugene, Oregon, my teaching partner for the past decade and coauthor with me of other books. "I seem to have a medical problem," she said in a voicemail. "Do you have any ideas?" I closed my eyes, still sitting by the telephone, and saw red and blue lines going up her arm to her shoulder and into her brain. I left a peculiar message on her machine describing what I had seen. In her return call, I learned that she had been stuck in the thumb by a rose thorn, and that her face and lips were feeling numb as a result. Based on that information, I urged her to go to the emergency room because it now sounded to me like blood poisoning. In the emergency room, she was given a tetanus shot and antibiotics, and she quickly recovered. Of course, since my patient was Jane, this might have simply been a case of mental telepathy. The distinction is that, in mental telepathy, I could have picked up Jane's mental impressions of her condition, which may or may not have been correct.

Forecasting

Jeffrey Mishlove and I both feel that the ability to forecast may be the most promising of all the applications of psychic faculties. Forecasting earthquakes, volcanic activity, political conditions, technological developments, weather conditions, interest rates, investment opportunities, and the prices of commodities and currencies constitutes an active and exciting area of study.

In 1982, I was part of a team of psychics and investors who wanted to see if it was possible to use psychic functioning to make money in the marketplace. We chose the silver market, and our highly successful efforts ended up on the front page of the *Wall Street Journal.* You can read more about this, and many other forecasting adventures, in the Associative Remote-Viewing section of Chapter 4.

"And we've just opened our brand new Gold Futures department."

THE SKEPTICS

When I related the Hearst story to my publisher, he asked why we didn't go after the $1,000,000 offered at that time by "The Amazing Randi" for any convincing demonstration of psychic abilities. Although I haven't the slightest doubt about the existence of these abilities and their usefulness, I have serious doubts about the likelihood of a lifelong professional skeptic paying up, no matter what evidence he saw.

There is an active skeptical organization in America called the Committee for the Scientific Investigation of Claims of the Paranormal (CSICOP; pronounced "psi-cop"), of which Randi is a prominent member. Their desire is to subtly encourage you to deny your own experience of psi when it appears, with the goal of "saving" science from psychical researchers. They don't do research, of course, and they don't particularly want to know the truth. Rather, they actively interfere with researchers' abilities to get money for their work. When given the opportunity, they waste the time of researchers and suck energy from the field. I give them as little attention as possible and, in spite of their efforts, I have had little trouble publishing my findings or getting research funds. I think it's a serious error to empower these enemies of truth, but some researchers are happy to immolate themselves on the pens of the critics, as long as someone pays attention to them.

From his lifelong experience in the field, Ingo Swann understands this problem well, and perfectly describes the tragic situation in his book *Natural ESP.* Ingo writes:

> Today it is a well-understood tactic of mind manipulation that if an unknown and unresolvable guilt can be established among a group of people (such as parapsychologists represent), that group can be controlled and subdued. As long as the target group accepts the possibility that the guilt might be true in some ways, it remains introverted and creatively unproductive. All its resources go into trying to resolve the "guilt" that does not exist in the first place.7

There is another organization whose members do not want to acknowledge psychic abilities. They are the ultimate secret keepers: the National Security Agency (NSA)! There are very few funny stories about the NSA, but two of them occurred in the first year of our research.

Shortly after we discovered that Ingo could describe distant locations given only their latitude and longitude, we proposed a demonstration to our friends at the CIA, who were already interested in our work. Hal was given a set of coordinates, which he read to Ingo. Ingo then began to describe and draw rolling hills, a curved driveway, a cluster of buildings, and an underground bunker. Pat Price was also at SRI at that time, and he offered to take a look at the site coordinates as well. He described psychically flying over the site at 5,000 feet to get a bird's-eye view (which I always ask viewers to do in remote-viewing sessions). He also made some detailed sketches. He then offered to "go inside" the bunker, where he found a file cabinet with names on the drawers. He read off the names, and gave us the code name ("Hay Stack") of the facility — all of which proved to be correct.

The coordinates were for a vacation cabin of the CIA agent with whom we were working. But, to his great surprise, just over the hill from his little house was an NSA microwave link and a code-breaking facility. When Price learned that he had described the "wrong" target (the NSA site, not the cabin), he told us, "The more you try to hide something, the more it shines like a beacon in psychic space."

This incident gave rise to an intense NSA investigation of us — Ingo, Pat, and the CIA agent. The NSA was not at all amused by the idea that the CIA would target one of their secret facilities with a bunch of California psychics. Pat mollified them somewhat by describing a similar Soviet microwave site in the Ural Mountains — a viewing that has since been confirmed.

As a result of this little adventure, we began to talk with the NSA about using ESP to crack codes. We made several trips to the "Puzzle Palace" at Fort Mead in Maryland to discuss what sort of coded message they would give us to unscramble (without having to show us an actual code). Since I have always believed that psi is limitless, I proposed that they give us a paragraph of text in their very best "unbreakable" code, seal it in metal foil, wrap it in black paper, and submit it to us as a secret document, which we would never open. We would just describe the ideas contained in the paragraph submitted — no need at all to see their silly cipher. Hal and I already had top-secret clearances, so this was not an outlandish proposal. We were just investigating and probing the limits of psi perception. In the military, however, they consider this kind of questioning to be "career limiting" if you don't already have answers. The top management at NSA was stunned by our proposal; even though we offered our services at no charge, they killed the experiment. They didn't want to know that psychics could read their code. Some people just have no sense of humor.

THE GANZFELD STUDIES

The NSA didn't want to know about remote viewing, but plenty of other people were pursuing psi research. Without a doubt, the most carefully and critically examined data that describe psi functioning are found in the Ganzfeld research. The Ganzfeld, meaning "whole field," is a controlled environment used in ESP research, in which all ordinary inputs to the psi subject are limited by sensory isolation. The Ganzfeld idea came out of the 1960s, when it was thought that altered states of consciousness would lead to more effective psychic functioning. We have since found that sensory isolation, flashing lights, hypnosis, and drugs are all unnecessary — and not even helpful.

The Ganzfeld studies investigate telepathic communication between a "sender" person and a "receiver" person. For more than fifteen years, this approach was pioneered by Charles Honorton at the Maimonides Hospital Research Center. Charles was an out-standing theoretician in psi research, as well as a humorous and congenial researcher. Regrettably, Charles died in 1992 at the early age of 46, depriving us of a great and compassionate seeker who devoted his entire career to the field of psychic research.

In 1994, after Honorton's death, a fifteen-page paper was pub-lished, coauthored by Honorton and psychologist Dr. Daryl Bem, a professor from Cornell University and a former skeptic. (Because they suffer from "physics envy," psychologists are the most skepti-cal of all academics.) The publication was a landmark accomplish-ment in the field of psi research because it appeared in the prestigious *Psychological Bulletin* of the American Psychological Association.[8] The experiments described in that paper were called "The Auto-Ganzfeld" because the researcher, sender, and receiver were all isolated from each other, and the researcher was isolated from the selection of the "target" videotapes, which were chosen and shown to the sender automatically by a computer.

In these experiments, the receiver was generally a volunteer from the community. The receiver was seated comfortably in a reclining chair in a soundproof room; Ping-Pong balls cut in half and taped over the receiver's eyes minimized visual distractions, while white noise (similar to the sound of ocean waves) was intro-duced via earphones. The receiver's task was to remain awake and to describe into a tape recorder all the impressions that passed through his or her mind during a thirty-minute session.

Meanwhile, a sender would be watching a randomly chosen two-minute videotape selection that was continuously repeated during the twenty-minute session. In some of these trials, the receivers' narrations were so accurate that it sounded as if they were watching the target videotape exactly as it was being shown to the senders! At the end of each trial, the computer that controlled the experiment would show the receiver the chosen segment and three other dummy video segments in random order. The receiver's task was to then decide which of the four mini-movies the sender had been watching. By chance, one would expect a 25-percent success rate in this process. In the entire set of eleven experimental series, which involved 240 people in 354 sessions, the hit rate was 32 percent, which departs from chance expectation by more than 500 to 1. Since the time of the Bem-Honorton publication, similar successful trials have been carried out with no sender. This is an example of pure clairvoyance — no mind-to-mind connection.

The Ganzfeld's Gifted Students

The most successful of the Auto-Ganzfeld studies was conducted by Charles Honorton in conjunction with Dr. Marilyn Schlitz, who went on to become the research director at the Institute of Noetic Sciences (IONS) in Petaluma, California. In 1991, Schlitz was working on a creativity research project with students at the Julliard School in New York. As part of this work, she enlisted twenty classical music and modern dance students to take part in a Ganzfeld study.[9] Each day, the students took the train from their urban campus on Broadway to the pastoral setting of the laboratory in Princeton. Apparently climbing off the railroad car into the grassy surroundings would itself initiate the New York City students' altered state. These talented and practiced artists, working in pairs with their friends in a laboratory setting, scored at a 50-percent rate in choosing the correct target from four possibilities. This is twice the rate one would expect by chance, and it was the highest rate of success described in the Bem-Honorton paper. It is comparable only to the success rate achieved between parents and their children in the Ganzfeld.

What We Know about Remote Viewing

For a phenomenon thought to be nonexistent by many people, we certainly know a great deal about remote viewing, including how to increase and decrease its accuracy and reliability. In the remainder of this chapter, I will share with you what we know about the process. Then, in Chapter 3, I will describe in detail how you can do remote viewing yourself.

Experiencing a Distant Location: Finding the Target

Remote viewers can often contact, experience, and describe what we call a "target" — a hidden object or a remote natural or architectural site, for example — based on geographical coordinates, the presence of a cooperative person at the location, or some other target description, which we call an "address." We have also shown that it is not necessary for anyone present at the viewing to know the correct address; it is sufficient to tell the viewer, "We have a target that needs a description."

Sensing the Targets

Inexperienced viewers are able to describe a target's shape, form, and color much more reliably than they can describe the target's function or provide other analytical information. In addition to visual imagery, viewers sometimes describe associated feelings, sounds, smells, and even electrical or magnetic fields. As a viewer, I have learned that if I see a color clearly and brightly, or something silver and shiny, that is the aspect of the target that I am most likely to describe correctly. It is even possible for viewers to experience aspects of a target that are not actually manifest, such as the color of an object inside an opaque box where there is no light.

Looking into the Future

Viewers can sense present, past, and even future activities at target sites. There is not a drop of evidence to indicate that it is more difficult for viewers to look slightly into the future than it is to describe an object in a box in front of them. In fact, at SRI we had the impression that our precognitive experiments tended to be more reliable that the real-time trials.

Accuracy and Reliability

Viewers can sometimes achieve photographic accuracy, and reliability in a series of experiments can be as high as 80 percent. Unlike card-guessing[10] or other forced-choice experiments, more than two decades of remote-viewing research have shown no decline in people's remote-viewing performance over time. It is the reliable source of psi — a kind of psychic battery — that researchers had sought for decades. With practice, people become increasingly able to separate the psychic signal from the mental noise of memory and imagination.

How Small Is Small?

Viewers have sensed targets and target details as small as one millimeter. Hella Hammid, one of our frequent research subjects, successfully described microscopic picture targets as small as one millimeter square in an experimental series at SRI in 1979. She also correctly identified a silver pin inside an aluminum film can.

In the 1890s, Annie Besant worked with psychic C. W. Leadbeater on an imaginative study to describe the structure of atoms. In this early research at the English Theosophical Society, Leadbeater was the first person in the world to describe the distinctive nuclear structure of the three isotopes of hydrogen. In his book *Occult Chemistry,* published in 1898, he described clairvoyantly seeing that, in paraffin, a given atom of hydrogen could have one, two, or three particles in its nucleus and still be hydrogen.[11] Isotopes had not yet been discovered by chemists, so Leadbeater was I believe the first to report that atoms of different atomic weights could retain their chemical identity.

Long-Distance Remote Viewing

Again and again, researchers have seen that accuracy and resolution in perceiving remote-viewing targets are not sensitive to
variations in distance of up to ten thousand miles. An example of
such long-distance viewing is an experiment Elisabeth Targ and I
did with the Russian healer Djuna Davitashvili in 1984. In this
Moscow-to-San Francisco remote viewing, Djuna was highly successful in focusing her attention not only six thousand miles to the
west, but two hours into the future. A similar, and now quite
famous, long-distance trial was undertaken by Pat Price in 1974,
when he successfully described a Soviet weapons factory at Semi-
palatinsk, in eastern Russia. We show these once-secret drawings
in *Miracles of Mind*.[12]

Electrical Shielding

"Faraday-cage" screen rooms and underwater shielding elimi-
nate almost all electromagnetic waves from the neighborhood, but
they have no negative effects on remote viewing. In fact, some
viewers prefer to work in an electrically shielded environment.
The well-known psychic Eileen Garrett showed me such a room
that she had built for her own use in her offices at the Parapsychology Foundation on 57th Street in New York City. Pat Price made
several fine descriptions of complex target sites from inside SRI's
shielded room. In 1978, Hella Hammid and Ingo Swann successfully received several messages sent from Palo Alto while they were
inside a submarine 500 miles away and 500 feet below the ocean's
surface.[13]

In fact, recent findings by physicist James Spottiswoode show
that electromagnetic radiation from our Milky Way galaxy and the
electromagnetic effects of solar flares both degrade psychic functioning.[14] Electrical shielding seems to help performance, and so
does carrying out experiments when the galactic radiation is at a

minimum at one's location. This occurs at 1,300 hours sidereal time[15] (star time, rather than sun time), but we find that it is still possible to be abundantly psychic at any time of the day or night.

Inhibiting Factors

Remote viewing is inhibited by prior knowledge of target possibilities, absence of feedback, or use of mental analysis. Lack of feedback prevents the viewer from looking into the future to precognitively see the target, thereby closing one of the important remote-viewing channels. Any visual or auditory distractions, or anything novel in the working environment, will tend to show up in the viewer's pictures during the remote-viewing session.

The nature of the target can also affect accuracy. Numbers are much more difficult to perceive than pictorial targets. For example, it is more difficult to guess a target number between one and ten than it is to describe a location chosen from an infinitude of planetary locations that one has never seen. This is because the viewer already has crystal-clear mental images of *all* the numbers, and these images from memory and imagination constitute significant mental noise.

Unfortunately, a psychic image does not come carrying a sign that says, "This picture is brought to you by ESP." That assessment must be made by the viewer.

Enhancing Factors

Seriousness of purpose, feedback after the trial, relaxation, acceptance of psi, and especially heart-to-heart trust among participants all enhance remote viewing. During the ESP learning phase, it is important to show the viewer the correct target after each trial. Without this trial-by-trial feedback, no learning takes place. Experienced viewers learn to improve their performance by becoming aware of their mental noise (from memory and imagination) and filtering it out. Performance is also improved when viewers write down their impressions and draw their mental pictures. Drawing is especially important, because it gives the viewer direct access to symbolic and nonanalytic unconscious processes.

Theoretical Considerations

It appears clear to us that viewers can focus their attention on distant points in space-time and then describe and experience those distant locations. Feedback is essential to learning, but with greater experience it is not necessary for psi functioning. In the phenomenon of remote viewing, it is as though the viewer is examining his or her own small, low-resolution, local piece of the four-dimensional space-time hologram in which he or she is embedded. Each little piece of the hologram contains all the information of the greater whole — but at a lower resolution. This is exactly the nonlocal connectivity that we discussed in Chapter 1.

FIRST-TIME EXPERIENCES OF THREE VIEWERS

You may be wondering if you can hope to achieve anything like accurate remote viewing yourself. In this section, I will tell the first-time stories of three people who acted as viewers in the remote-viewing trials at SRI: Pat Price, Joe McMoneagle, and Hella Hammid. All three were interested in remote viewing and psychic abilities, but none of them had formally pursued that interest before meeting Hal and me. The results we obtained with them are typical of what we saw at SRI, as well as in the remote viewing workshops Jane Katra and I offer to equally inexperienced people.

Pat Price

Pat Price is the retired policeman I mentioned earlier in this chapter, who helped the Berkeley police in their search for Patty

Hearst. In Pat's first attempt at remote viewing at SRI, he made a psychic drawing of a swimming pool complex five miles from the viewing site. He was able to specify the dimensions, size, location, and function of a round pool, a rectangular pool, and the adjacent buildings, to an accuracy of 90 percent.

Joe McMoneagle

Another beginning research subject, Joe McMoneagle, was able to draw a detailed picture of a location where a CIA agent was hiding, one hundred miles from SRI. He drew a shockingly accurate picture of a T-shaped, six-story building covered with glass, adjacent to a line of trees — our very own atomic bomb factory in Livermore, California. (You can see some of the drawings by Pat Price and Joe McMoneagle on my Website: http://www.espresearch.com and in *Miracles of Mind.*)

Hella Hammid

SRI's great success with Ingo Swann, Pat Price, and Joe McMoneagle eventually caused our government sponsors to request that we find a subject with even less remote-viewing experience than these three. They wanted a so-called "control subject." We brought in Hella Hammid, a dear longtime friend of mine from New York. When Hella first came into the SRI program in 1974, she said she had no previous psi experience but was excited about the challenge.

Hella had been a regular photography contributor to *Life* and many other magazines since the 1950s. I was fortunate to have such a wise and openhearted woman as a test subject in psi research, as she became our most reliable viewer for more than a decade. Hella died in 1992, but she is often in my thoughts as I continue the work that we did together.

Figure 4. Artist and psychic Ingo Swann (left) with photographer Hella Hammid. Hammid entered the SRI program as a "control" subject and turned out to be one of its most reliable viewers. Photo by Hal Puthoff.

Inside Hella's First Session

Hella's first session at SRI is a good illustration of how a remote-viewing session functions. My partner Hal Puthoff drove to an unknown and randomly chosen target location; Hella's job was to describe where he had gone. I sat on the floor of our laboratory while Hella settled herself on the couch and asked me, "What do I do?" I didn't know how to answer Hella's question at the time, but the answer has since become a large part of this book, particularly the following chapter.

Remote viewing can be done without an interviewer, but we now know that our remote-viewing success derived in part from the rapport between the remote viewer and the interviewer, acting as an information-gathering team. The remote viewer's role is that of perceiver and information channel. The interviewer's role is that of an analytical control — from my point of view, a kind of "psychic travel agent."

This division of labor mirrors the two primary modes of cerebral functioning as we understand them: the *nonanalytical* thinking style that predominates in spatial pattern recognition and other holistic processing (which is thought to predominate in psi functioning), and the *analytical* cognitive style that characterizes verbal and other goal-oriented reasoning processes. Only very experienced remote viewers appear to have the ability to handle both cognitive styles simultaneously without an interviewer.

After all, even the priestess working as the Oracle at Delphi in ancient Greece had an interviewer. As she sat on her tripod in the Temple of Apollo, the priest would ask her questions relating to the information sought by the customer who wanted to know the future, whether it was a merchant or a king.[16] Her ramblings would then be unscrambled and put into hexameter verse — the form expected by the customer — much as we at SRI would write a remote-viewing report for the CIA.

In that first session with Hella, I asked her to relax for a couple of minutes. I didn't tell her how to relax; it doesn't seem to matter. What matters is becoming present in the moment of time and space of the experiment — to leave shopping, driving, and kids behind.

"Now that your eyes are closed and you're relaxed," I said, "can you tell me about your mental pictures regarding where Hal is located now? Do not *guess* where he might be," I told her. "Just describe what you see or what you are experiencing."

"I see motion," Hella said. "Something is moving along fast." This type of kinesthetic input often comes before knowing. I asked her to make a sketch of her first impression of whatever was moving. She made the little drawing at the bottom of Figure 5. In remote viewing, we consider these first impressions to be invaluable, as they often set the tone for the whole viewing experience.

PEDESTRIAN OVERPASS

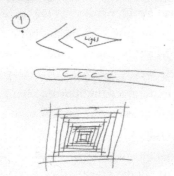

Figure 5. Hella Hammid's first remote viewing. The target (top) was a pedestrian overpass. Hella's drawings are shown below.

I then invited Hella to take a break, open her eyes, and breathe. People often start to hold their breath when they are doing remote viewing, which is neither necessary nor helpful. Taking a break is an essential ingredient of successful remote viewing; it provides an opportunity to clean the mental slate so that the viewer can return to the target and obtain fresh and different information.

Without an interviewer, however, a viewer tends to hold on to the first image, even when it probably would not help identify the target. For example, if I get a clear and surprising mental picture of a daffodil at an outdoor target, I may feel very pleased — even though it would not be at all helpful to a judge or policeman trying to locate a crime target.

After Hella's one-minute break, I asked her to tell me about any new mental pictures that came to view. Through all this, I had no idea what the target was; this was a double-blind experiment, as all of our experiments have been. As a result, I could say anything I wished to Hella; I had absolutely no information to communicate, except about the process.

In her second look at the target, Hella said she saw "some kind of trough up in the air. But it can't hold water because it is full of holes." We then took another break.

Because of the magical and highly charged nature of this process, an interviewer can often remember exactly what the viewer says in a session. In the early stages of a remote-viewing session, the interviewer can say very few kinds of things to a viewer without introducing mental noise and introducing an analytic element of guessing. An interviewer can nondirectively say, "Tell me more about what you are experiencing" or "What else do you see?" Or, if a viewer makes a guess at the nature or name of a target, an interviewer should ask, "What are you experiencing that makes you say [repeat whatever was said]? How do you feel about this place?" It is often particularly useful to ask the viewer to look for new or surprising elements that don't seem to make sense.

Finally, I asked Hella, if she could "stand where Hal is standing, and describe what he is seeing."

"This is very complicated," she said, "I have to make a drawing. It looks like squares within squares within squares."

She then made the third drawing in Figure 5.

The target was the pedestrian overpass across the freeway, at Oregon Avenue in Palo Alto. This trial was one of a series of nine that were successful at odds of almost one in a million. Out of nine trials, Hella had five first-place matches and four second-place matches in blind judging. (In blind judging, a "judge," who does not know the correct answers, has to decide which of Hella's nine descriptions goes with each one of the nine targets.)

RESULTS FROM REMOTE-VIEWING WORKSHOPS

When Jane Katra and I teach workshops, we use beautiful colored photographs of outdoor locations as targets for the remote viewers. We teach everyone to be both a viewer and an interviewer. In a typical session half the people are viewers, and their workshop partners for the day become their interviewers. Each person has his or her unique picture sealed in an envelope, and I provide general guidance as we go along.

A case in point was our third trip to the city of Arco, in northern Italy, where we had twenty-four people in our class. I am very fond of this beautiful Alpine town — the mountains in the background, the warmhearted affectionate people, and the fact that every conversation begins with a hug and a kiss on both cheeks. There is no fear of intimacy here; it's easy to feel psychic.

"Describe your mental image pertaining to the picture in the envelope," I ask students. Or, I might say, "Describe the picture that you will see in ten minutes, when you open the envelope." The latter instruction is often helpful because it invites the viewer to make use of the ever-present precognitive channel, in addition to the real-time clairvoyance of the present.

At the end of the session, each viewer and interviewer is shown an identical copy of the target picture, along with three randomly chosen nontarget (dummy) pictures. (The actual target picture — the picture the viewer was trying to visualize and draw — is still in the envelope.) The interviewer is then asked to choose which one of the four pictures the viewer has been describing, based solely on that description. In each of our three Italian workshops and one of my own in 2003, we have had a hitting rate of at least 66 percent first-place matches, where only 25 percent would be expected by chance. This equates to odds of better than one in a thousand for each workshop.

We have not done nearly this well in the U.S., especially in Silicon Valley, although we're working with exactly the same target materials. This is interesting, and we don't know why it's so. It may have something to do with the constant self-judgment we're accustomed to exercising here: "Am I doing it right?" By contrast, Italian women are open and self-confident; they know they're beautiful and sexy, so why not psychic?

I also suspect that our four U.S. groups have a greater fear of intimacy and surrender than the people of northern Italy. There is an aspect of remote viewing that is like making love; it requires complete surrender to the task at hand, with no preconception or self-judgment about the outcome. It also requires control of one's awareness to achieve what Patanjali calls "a single-pointed focus of attention."

Viewer Dynamics

Even though their target is only a picture, viewers have mobility; they are free to drift around the target. When they do so, they often see things that are not shown in the picture but which, in fact, exist. (This sometimes makes it difficult for the interviewer, who must later determine which of several pictures a viewer was trying to describe; the interviewer has only the picture to use for evaluation.)

In an Arco workshop, an architect viewer was having trouble getting any mental pictures at all. Finally, in my last invitation to the group, I said, "Why don't each of you drift up in the air and look down on the target?" With this, the architect began to sketch busily.

For the architect, the target picture was the Parthenon in Greece. In Figure 6, we see in the viewer's drawing that the columns of the temple have all been laid flat, with their locations indicated by dots inside the rectangle. This kind of dynamic activity is often seen in remote-viewing drawings.

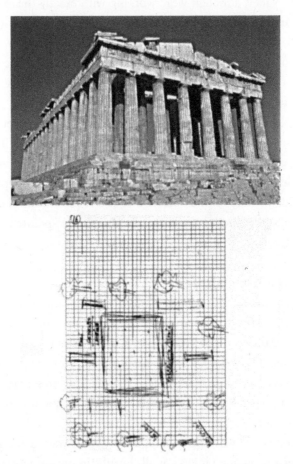

Figure 6. The target picture of the Parthenon (top) and a fragmented drawing by an architect participating in a remote-viewing workshop in Arco, Italy.

Ingo Swann devotes a whole chapter to this kind of distortion in his excellent book *Natural ESP*. He calls it "lack of fusion," and from his own experience he gives four degrees of distortion:

1. All parts are correctly perceived, but will not connect to form a whole.
2. Some parts are fused, while others are not.
3. Fusion is only approximate.
4. Parts are incorrectly fused; all parts are there, but put together in such a way as to falsely create another image.

René Warcollier also discusses this phenomenon in his groundbreaking book, *Mind-to-Mind*.[17] Warcollier describes this distortion as a kind of "parallelism," in which similar geometric elements rearrange themselves:

> What seems to happen in the case of geometric figures is that movement is injected into what would otherwise be a static image. It is almost as if we had for telepathy no memory trace of specific geometric figures, such as the rectangle and the circle. Instead we possess only angles and arcs. There is a sort of mutual attraction between suitable parts, a kind of grouping, which I call "the law of parallelism."

From his hundreds of picture-drawing trials, Warcollier gives six illustrations of this parallelism, or "lack of fusion" effect. These are shown in Figure 7.

Warcollier had great insight into the psychic perception problem. He (and, later, Ingo Swann) taught that mental analysis, memory, and imagination constitute a kind of mental noise in the remote-viewing channel. Therefore, the closer the viewer can get to raw, uninterpreted imagery and experience, the better. The viewer is encouraged to report spontaneous perceptions ("What are you experiencing now?" "What are you seeing that makes you say such-and-such?") rather than analyze, since the naked, direct experience tends to be on target, while the analysis is usually incorrect. Memory, analysis, and imagination are the enemies of psychic functioning.

Figure 7. René Warcollier's *Mind-to-Mind* experiments demonstrating lack of fusion.

STAGES OF REMOTE VIEWING

Ingo Swann introduced all of us at SRI to the great potential of remote viewing, and he spent many years developing theories about this ability. Swann feels that one passes through distinct stages in a remote-viewing session as one accesses increasingly detailed and analytical information. The first stage of remote viewing consists primarily of kinesthetic sensations and initial fragmentary images that can be sketched. Joe McMoneagle calls this the "major gestalt stage."

Stage-two experiences involve basic emotional and aesthetic sensations of the target, such as fear, loneliness, or a sense of beauty. Joe points out that this is where we notice that our perception is "like" something. It is not the thing, but it is like it. In this situation, it's a good idea to ask, "How do you *feel* about this object (or place)?"

Dimensional descriptions, such as "large," "heavy," or "thin," comprise stage three. At this point, viewers often get strong urges to make free-form sketches, the meaning of which may not be apparent to them. Viewers are often tempted to make analytical guesses about the name or function of the target. Swann calls these labels "analytical overlay," or "AOL." Saying that your mental picture is "like" something is a way of indicating your awareness of AOL. Swann encourages viewers to develop an awareness of this mental noise, and to avoid the intellectualization of naming and guessing. Dzogchen teachers call this tendency to name or analyze "conditioned existence," as compared with "naked awareness."

Information that actually describes the target's function or purpose forms the basis of stage four, during which Swann teaches his viewers to write detailed lists of their perceptions. The last bits of physical and functional descriptors are combined in a final sketch that identifies the target. Joe assures us that, at this stage, "the hidden aspects of the target will begin to shine through," and we can learn to recognize them.

I believe that if you take the time to follow the exercises I provide in the following chapter, you can learn to successfully pass through each of these stages of remote viewing. Then you will be able to use these abilities in your daily life.

for your viewing

pleasure

HOW YOU CAN PRACTICE REMOTE VIEWING

We all have the gift of expanded awareness, or ESP. In this chapter, I will first discuss several aspects of successful remote-viewing, then take you through a process of remote-viewing practice step-by-step.

The only limits to our psychic abilities are the mental noise of memory, imagination, and analysis. In this chapter, I will also describe this mental chatter and introduce the techniques we have developed for overcoming it.

There is a continuum of psychic experiences available to everyone. At one end of the spectrum is the peaceful remote-viewing practice I teach, in which one can "see" and describe distant scenes on one's mental screen. At the other end of the spectrum are out-of-body experiences, in which one travels mentally to a distant place, bringing along as much sensitivity, emotionality, and sexuality[1] as one can comfortably manage.

"No cause for alarm, folks. I'm Morey Kranshaw, from down the block, and I'm having an out-of-body experience."

© The *New Yorker Collection* 1978 Lee Lorenz from cartoonbank.com. All Rights Reserved.

We did not teach out-of-body travel at SRI; we didn't want anyone to complain to the management — or the government — that we had separated their consciousness from their body and that they couldn't put themselves back together again!

Jane Katra and I have had the great pleasure and privilege of showing hundreds of people all over the world how to become remote viewers — how to get in touch with the part of themselves that is psychic. Over the past three years, we have conducted several workshops in Italy, ending each with a formal, double-blind test of participants' remote-viewing abilities. These demonstrations showed a highly significant departure from chance expectation — better than one in a thousand (three results in a row like this beats odds of one in a billion).[2] We are confident that by the end of this chapter you, too, will have learned this skill.

MENTAL NOISE

Ingo Swann has written extensively on the ways in which we distort our perceived psychic images in our efforts at remote viewing.

As mentioned in the previous chapter, "analytical overlay" (AOL) is his term for the process of contaminating our direct experience of a target with our analysis of the images based on our imagination and memories of similar images. The unconscious naming of the images on our mental screen causes this mental noise. In the Dzogchen Buddhist tradition, this naming, guessing, or grasping is called "conditioned awareness."

This powerful, and usually subconscious, mental conditioning is caused by our association with friends, society, education, and childhood training and indoctrination. We know from research in perceptual psychology that what we consciously experience is the ratio of the perceived signal to the mental and environmental noise. In other words, the less "noise" we have, the more accurate our perceptions will be. We do not know how to increase the psychic signal strength in remote viewing, but over the years we have become skillful in helping students reduce and overcome the sources of mental noise that interfere with and degrade psychic ability. By avoiding naming and analysis, and by becoming aware of our lifetime conditioning, we can learn to view with naked awareness and greatly increase the signal-to-noise ratio of our process. When people successfully gain this awareness, it is often a life-changing experience for them, going well beyond an improved ability to find their car keys.

As we learn to see the world without this conditioning, we experience it undistorted, with naked awareness. There is a ninth-century Dzogchen teaching on exactly this subject. It is called "self-liberation through seeing with naked awareness."[3] The sage who brought the Dzogchen teachings to Tibet was Padmasambhava. On the subject of direct perception, he wrote:

> Thus, things are perceived in various different ways, and may be elucidated in various different ways.
> Because you grasped at these various [appearances that

arise], becoming attached to them, errors have come into existence. Yet with respect to all these appearances of which you are aware in your mind, even though these appearances that you perceive do arise, if you do not grasp at them, then that is Buddhahood. Appearances are not erroneous in themselves, but because of your grasping, errors come into existence.

Even though the entire external inanimate universe appears to you, it is but a manifestation of mind.

Therefore your own manifest self-awareness comes to see everything nakedly. This self-liberation through seeing with "naked awareness" is a direct introduction to one's own intrinsic awareness [of who you are].[4]

From our research at SRI, we know that the entire external universe can, indeed, come into view. In the Dzogchen literature, this is called "naked awareness" or "intrinsic awareness," and is the portal to self-realization. Twelve hundred years later, we call it remote viewing.

CHOOSING TARGET OBJECTS

Selecting good targets is an extremely important part of the remote-viewing process. There are many kinds of objects you can choose as targets. Some of these will be easier to describe remotely than others. The goal in choosing a target for practice is to make the whole process as easy and successful as possible. The target object should be bigger than a matchbox and smaller than a bread box. It should be visually interesting and have describable parts, rather than being compact. That is, a Raggedy-Ann doll or a teacup with a handle is easier to describe than an ivory Buddha figurine or a tennis ball. A pineapple would be easier to describe than a peach. A hairbrush is better than a nail file. A remote-viewing object should be attractive and worth describing: no lumps of coal or number-two pencils. It's also best to avoid using a target object that might be perceived as frightening or distasteful to the viewer. This is an important point, since you would not want to violate your viewer's unconditional trust of you or the process.

DESCRIBING HIDDEN OBJECTS

I want to make practicing remote viewing as easy as possible, so rather than ask you to collect interesting pictures or hide a person or object at a distant location, I suggest that you use small objects hidden in opaque containers as targets for remote-viewing practice.

As an example, I will describe some simple, successful experiments in which Hal and I asked Hella Hammid to describe the appearance of some small concealed objects. We wanted to know if it was possible to describe the color of an object inside an aluminum 35-millimeter film can. There is no light in such a can, of course, and we were interested in the perception of a colored object when the color was not manifest.

I did not know the contents of the ten cans that we provided. In our experiment, Hal would randomly choose a sealed can each day and take it to the park across the street from our laboratory. I would then interview Hella regarding her psychic impressions of the contents of the can — what she thought she would see coming out of the can in half an hour when she opened it. When the target was a spool of thread and a pin with a head, she made the drawing at the top of Figure 8, describing a nail with a head. When the object was a curled-up leaf, she drew spirals and talked of a nautilus shell. When we had a tiny key-ring belt, Hella expressed surprise that one could "get a belt into a film can." In retrospect, I think that one of the targets — a can full of sand — was a poor remote viewing choice since it has no shape apart from the can it is in.

Figure 8 shows the first five cans and their contents. Hella made four first-place matches and one second-place match (the can of sand). What we learned from this experiment is that a viewer can psychically see an object as small as a pin from a quarter of a mile away, and can apparently describe colors as well.

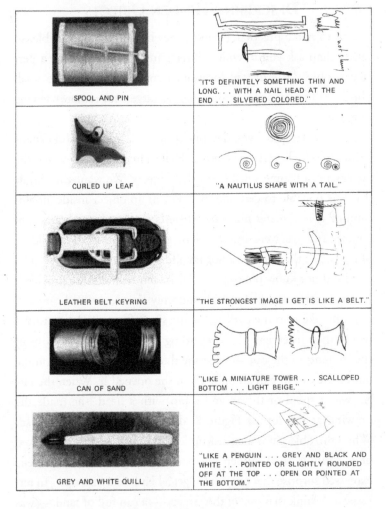

SPOOL AND PIN

"IT'S DEFINITELY SOMETHING THIN AND LONG. . . WITH A NAIL HEAD AT THE END . . . SILVERED COLORED."

CURLED UP LEAF

"A NAUTILUS SHAPE WITH A TAIL."

LEATHER BELT KEYRING

"THE STRONGEST IMAGE I GET IS LIKE A BELT."

CAN OF SAND

"LIKE A MINIATURE TOWER . . . SCALLOPED BOTTOM . . . LIGHT BEIGE."

GREY AND WHITE QUILL

"LIKE A PENGUIN . . . GREY AND BLACK AND WHITE . . . POINTED OR SLIGHTLY ROUNDED OFF AT THE TOP . . . OPEN OR POINTED AT THE BOTTOM."

Figure 8. Hella Hammid's film-can experiment: four first-place matches and one second-place match (the can of sand).

Hella Hammid taught us much of what we understand about the potential of remote viewing. During her nine trials of viewing distant geographical targets, she achieved a rating even more statistically significant than Pat Price's highly successful similar series. We conducted successive studies in which Hella accurately described objects hidden in wooden boxes or aluminum film cans, and even microscopic targets the size of a dot (micro-dots), such as those used by spies to conceal messages in letters. All these viewings were carefully evaluated by blind judging, as described in Chapter 2, and found to be statistically significant as well. So, in the end, our inexperienced control subject became our most extensively published SRI psychic!

THE VIEWER AND THE SURROUNDINGS

Hella was a cautious viewer in that she did not elaborate on her descriptions beyond what she actually saw and felt psychically. Pat Price, on the other hand, went to extremes to give highly detailed architectural descriptions of target sites. These were usually correct, but occasionally they were entirely off the mark. We would definitely not say that one viewer was more psychic than the other. Rather, we would say that they had different styles. If a terrorist had planted a bomb somewhere in the city, I would probably call Pat to try to find it. If I had lost my keys somewhere in the house, I would call Hella to describe what piece of furniture they had fallen behind.

Remote viewing can sometimes be challenging because it requires the full attentive powers of the remote viewer.[5] The environment and procedures involved with remote viewing are designed to be natural and comfortable so as to minimize the diversion of attention to anything other than the task at hand. No hypnosis, strobe lights, sensory-deprivation procedures, or drugs are used since, in our view, such novel environmental factors would divert some of the subject's much-needed attention. Our experience suggests that novice viewers following the simple procedures suggested in this book should be able to develop their psychic abilities without giving away their minds or having to eat porridge at the feet of a guru.

Whether remote viewing is done with or without an interviewer, it is important to recognize that remote viewing involves a division of labor between perception and analysis. The remote viewer's responsibility is confined to exercising the remote-viewing faculty. The viewer must describe and experience his or her mental pictures — without judging or analyzing them.

THE INTERVIEWER'S ROLE

It is the interviewer's responsibility (not the remote viewer's) to see that the necessary information is generated to permit an impartial judge to discriminate among the target descriptions. In the published literature, the most successful remote-viewing series have all involved interviewers, and the viewers have always had immediate feedback as to what the correct target was. In any human undertaking, there is no learning without feedback.

The interviewer has much more latitude to ask questions when the target is an object than when it is a location. Since the interviewer tries hard not to ask leading questions, places can be very limiting. But with objects that will be in the viewer's hand at a later time for feedback, the interviewer can ask a range of questions. For example:

- What does this object look like in your hand?
- How does it feel?
- Is it shiny or colored?
- Does it have much weight?

- What do you feel you could do with this object?
- What does it feel like when you squeeze it?
- Mentally turn it over; does something new come into view?
- Does it have an odor?

In our experiment, we had Hal go to the park with the object because if we put the object in a bag on the table in front of the viewer, the viewer would try to "see" into it — like Superwoman trying to see through the bag with X-ray vision. That approach doesn't appear to work; it's not remote viewing.

Often, a viewer will say, "I see something like a fire hydrant." This generally means that the viewer is not, in fact, seeing a fire hydrant. This is a good time for the interviewer to ask, "What are you experiencing (seeing) that makes you think of a fire hydrant?" The remote viewer is encouraged to sketch and write down everything he or she sees, despite objections of not being an artist or being unable to sketch. The viewer may record impressions throughout, or may wait until the end of the session if intermittent drawing would disrupt concentration. Since drawings tend to be more accurate than verbalizations, this is an extremely important factor for generating positive results.

REMOTE VIEWING WITHOUT AN INTERVIEWER

Although we emphasize how helpful it is to have an interviewer working with the remote viewer to perform the analytic part of the task, it is not essential. Experienced viewers can ask themselves the questions as they go along. However, if you are working alone, it is still necessary that you find a way to prepare targets in a blind fashion.

Another example from our experience at SRI will illustrate the process of remote viewing without an interviewer. One of the brightest and most engaging "contract monitors" sent to us from the CIA was a young woman with a Ph.D. in mechanical engineering, whom I will call "Dr. P." She was very curious about the potential of ESP. Dr. P. told me that she had joined the CIA immediately after getting her degree and reading *Psychic Discoveries Behind the Iron Curtain* because she felt sure that the CIA must have an extensive psychic research program similar to what Ostrander and Schroeder described in that book.[6] She was right.

By 1976, we'd already had a physician and a physicist as contract monitors. But when Dr. P. showed up, we were in for something different. She brought a more hands-on approach. "I sent two guys out to California to visit you, and after a week they come back and they think they're psychic. I want to go over the whole protocol myself," she said.

We were happy to oblige her, and found her very entertaining. She was an attractive woman with long, dark hair who, for a reason we never discovered, frequently arrived at our laboratory at 9:00 A.M. wearing a beautiful party dress — quite different from what we were accustomed to at SRI.

She wanted to be treated just like the other remote viewers in the program in order to see where we had slipped up — or perhaps fooled her envoys. She did two remote-viewing trials in which she turned in excellent drawings and descriptions of the randomly chosen target locations where Hal had gone to hide. In both of these trials, I was the interviewer.

The morning after these trials, Dr. P. had a new plan. She wanted to do the remote viewing by herself — no interviewer. After all, she proposed, I might have known the answer all along and encouraged or led her in the correct direction. That made sense. So we gave her the tape recorder and some paper and left her in our laboratory suite. We thoroughly taped the door closed after we left because we didn't trust her either!

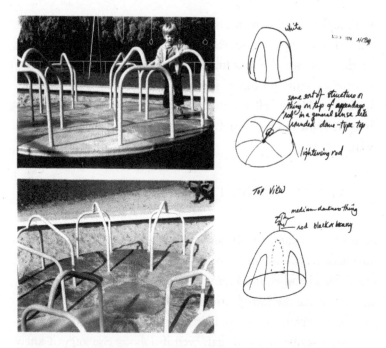

Figure 9. Target photos of a merry-go-round (left) and a CIA viewer's drawings. The viewer worked alone, with no interviewer.

Our electronic random-number generator chose a target envelope, out of sixty possibilities, that sent us to the merry-go-round at Rinconada Park, five miles from SRI. We went to the park, took pictures, and made a tape recording of the little children on the merry-go-round calling out, "Push me, push me." When we returned to SRI thirty minutes later, the door was still taped shut and Dr. P. was hunched over in the corner of the room. She had spent most of the time with her hands over her ears because she was concerned that there might be subliminal clues coming from hidden speakers in the walls. Although she was passionately interested in psi, she was equally determined not to be deceived by us!

She had drawn a circular object divided into six wedges and situated on a central rod, just like the merry-go-round. There were arches on the main disc, and she thought the whole thing was called a "cupola," although she wasn't sure what a cupola was; neither were we. We now know that a cupola is the circular, decorative structure on top of some Russian, Italian, and Victorian buildings. Her excellent, and unassisted, remote-viewing drawings are shown in Figure 9. Our contract was renewed for another year.

VIEWERS NEEDN'T ALWAYS DRAW PICTURES

In 1975, Hal and I were looking for financial support for our fledgling ESP program. I had the idea to call Richard Bach, who had just become famous for his book *Jonathan Livingston Seagull*.7 My good friend and editor, Eleanor Friede, was also Richard's editor, and she made the introductions. I called Richard at his home on top of an airplane hanger in Florida. I told him about our remote-viewing research and said that, even if nobody else knew, I knew his book wasn't really about a bird at all but, rather, about a person having an out-of-body experience. I asked if he would like to come to California and learn to do remote viewing and, if he enjoyed it, possibly help support our research. (When people ask me about career opportunities in psi research, I tell them about this kind of cold-call for funding.)

One crisp fall day, Richard arrived at SRI. We told him that Hal would go hide somewhere in the San Francisco Bay Area, and he and I would stay in the lab and describe Hal's site. At the appointed time, I guided Richard to describe his mental pictures regarding Hal's location. Richard said he couldn't draw, but that he saw a big inverted V-shape: a very tall building. I invited him to drift into the building and describe what was there. He said it was like an airport terminal. The use of "like" is always a key that a memory is being triggered, so I asked him to tell me what he was experiencing that made him say "airport terminal." He said, "I see a long, open space. At the end is the ticket counter — a long white counter. And behind the counter, on the wall, is the logo of the company."

The target was a large, A-frame Methodist church in Palo Alto, with a long white marble altar at the end of the building. And sure enough, on the wall, behind the altar was "the logo of the company": a cross. When Richard visited the church with us, he was very happy — and he gave us a generous check to help with our research.

MIND-TO-MIND VS. DOUBLE-BLIND

When I teach remote viewing, I always like the first two trials to include the possibility of a telepathic — mind-to-mind — channel between the interviewer and the viewer. In order for this to occur, the interviewer needs to know what the target object is, unlike the conditions of a double-blind trial. This gives the viewer three possible paths for receiving psychic data:

- The direct clairvoyant connection to the target object
- The telepathic connection with the interviewer, who already knows the target object
- The precognitive channel to the future moment when the interviewer puts the object into the viewer's hand

However, if the interviewer knows the target there is always a possibility of giving subconscious cues as to the correctness of the viewer's description or drawing during the session. This could make for a bad outcome; the viewer would be learning to read the interviewer's breathing and tone of voice, and learning nothing about psychic and mental processes. Experts like Ingo Swann believe that, in the early stages, learning remote viewing can be enhanced by having an interviewer who knows the target. On the

other hand, Joe McMoneagle, in his book *Remote Viewing Secrets,*
suggests that "all persons present should be blind to the target."[8]
So what should we do?

When Jane Katra and I teach remote-viewing workshops, our
first rule is that remote viewing should be fun. One of the fun
exercises we give our students evolved out of a need to entertain
ourselves during our extensive travels together: exchanging mental
pictures. This is a very simple game. One person holds an image
of an object in mind, and the other person describes the image it
conjures up. This channel can work so well that it would be a pity
to deprive yourself of the experience in the early stages of learning
remote viewing. After a few such trials, however, we believe you
should work in a double-blind situation, in which the interviewer
doesn't know the answer.

You can do this by having the interviewer thoroughly mix
up the containers or shopping bags that hold the target objects so
that she or he doesn't know what any one particular container
holds. Then the interviewer can take one of the containers and put
it on a table in another room, out of sight. You are then ready to
begin a double-blind trial.

GETTING STARTED

Now that much of the mystery has been revealed, you should be
able to practice remote viewing with a friend and learn to come
into contact with the part of yourself that is psychic.

Here is a step-by-step example of how to do remote viewing
with a partner; as I've noted, this seems to bring about the best
results.

1.   Have a friend choose an interesting object from
     around the house and put it into a bag on a table in
     another room. This will be your target object.

Before you begin the remote viewing, the interviewer should sit with you in a dimly lit room, and each of you should have a pen and paper. Write the date and your name on the top of a page, along with the phrase "I can do remote viewing." This is your affirmation for success. After twenty or thirty remote viewings, you can think about skipping the affirmation if you want to. But always write "Target for [today's date]" as an indication of your seriousness of purpose.

Take a few minutes to quiet your mind, breathing deeply and slowly, letting thoughts arise and pass away, until your mind is clear of mental chatter and you feel calm.

REMEMBER: According to Warcollier and Swann, mental analysis, memory, guessing, and imagination constitute a kind of mental noise in the remote-viewing channel.

Your interviewer might say something like, "I have an object that needs a description." (This is the object the interviewer has already put into a bag for you.)

REMEMBER: The remote viewer's role is that of perceiver and information channel. The interviewer's role is to draw out the information, not to analyze it. The direct experience tends to be on target, while the analysis is usually incorrect.

There must be complete trust between the viewer and the interviewer. Remote viewing is a peaceful and surrendered activity. The interviewer is not judging the viewer's performance.

2. Close your eyes, relax for a couple of minutes, and tell the interviewer about your mental pictures relating to the object, starting with the very first fragmentary shapes or forms. These first psychic bits are the most important shapes you will see.

REMEMBER: First impressions and shapes are invaluable; they often set the tone for the whole viewing experience.

Your interviewer continues: "Now that your eyes are closed and you're relaxed, can you tell me about your mental pictures regarding the item located in the other room?"

3. Tell the interviewer what you see on your mental screen. Write down your answers, or have the interviewer write them down for you word for word.

If you had a sharp, clear impression before you started this session, tell the interviewer what you saw. It is essential to "debrief" the images that come with you into a session; they may have nothing to do with the target. Sharp, clear images at the start of a session must be spoken out loud in order to clean your mental slate of this kind of analytical noise.

4. Sketch the very first fragmentary shapes or forms.

You should make little sketches of these images as they come to view, even if they don't make sense or are not really objects. Your hand may make little movements in the air over the paper; notice them and describe what your subliminal mind is trying to tell you. Relax and say what comes to you. Your interviewer will be listening intently and acting as a memory bank for your descriptions, so you are free to simply "see" and describe the images that come into view.

5. Good. Now take a short break.

6. When you are ready, look again at your internal mental slate. Remember to breathe after each new picture emerges. You may "see," or be given, another bit of psychic information — more shapes or forms — or you may be shown more of the "picture" you have already seen.

As a viewer, you are especially looking for surprising and novel images that do not belong to your normal repertoire of mental images.

Your interviewer can continue to keep you focused with questions such as:

- What are you experiencing now?
- How do you feel about the target?
- Are there any new or surprising elements?
- What are you seeing that makes you say such-and-such?

REMEMBER: The use of "like" is always a key that a memory is being triggered. Your interviewer should follow up with further related questions.

7. In your mind, hold the imaginary target object in your hand for a few minutes.

Your interviewer can now ask the following questions while you describe the object:

- Does it have a color?
- Is it shiny?
- Does it have sharp edges?
- What could you do with it?
- Does it have movable parts?
- Does it have an odor?
- Is it heavy or light, wood or metal?

When you begin to work with outdoor targets, you also will look for motion at the site. In addition, you can go into the distant target or drift in the air above it for a valuable bird's-eye view.

When you have finished, begin again. You should continue this quiet mental process until no new bits of information come to you. The whole process should not take more than ten to fifteen minutes.

REMEMBER: To be right, you have to be willing to be wrong. This is why the issue of trust between viewer and interviewer is so important.

Through this process, you can learn to give a surprisingly coherent description of a hidden object. You are exceedingly unlikely, however, to know exactly what the object is.

8. After you have described a number of images of this target, summarize all the things you have said.

Try to specify the images that you feel most strongly about and decide whether each one is more likely to have arisen from memory (perhaps things you saw earlier in the day) or imagination. That is, when you are through viewing, you must go through your notes and sketches and separate out the psychic bits from the analytical noise. The collection of psychic bits will be your description of the target.

If you had been told in advance that your target would be one of two or more objects, it would greatly increase the difficulty of describing the correct target because you would have mental pictures of all the items in your mind. To separate out the psychic bits of information from the analytical overlay (mental noise), you may still have to go through the bit-collecting process many times. So we recommend that you aren't told about multiple objects in advance. (To the best of my knowledge, Ingo Swann is the only person who can reliably discriminate between known targets; he was correct 80 percent of the time in formal SRI experiments!)

9. After you have made your sketches and written down your impressions, your interviewer should show you the object and go over with you the things you correctly described.

During this step, you may have the experience of saying, "I saw one of those but I didn't mention it!" as often happens. The rule in the remote-viewing game is that if it didn't get down on the paper, it didn't happen. So it is important to write down or draw everything; eventually you will learn to separate the signal from the noise.

We often say that psi is like musical ability: it is widely distributed in the population, and everyone has some ability and can participate to some extent — in the same way that the most nonmusical person can learn to play a little Mozart on the piano. On the other hand, there is no substitute for innate talent, and there is no substitute for practice.

I hope that this chapter has helped you get started in developing your psi abilities. More importantly, I hope it gives you permission to express and use all your innate abilities and gifts. Based on three decades of experience, I have no doubt that you can do remote viewing if you follow these instructions. No secret ingredient has been omitted. I wish you success — and the feelings of excitement and awe that accompany it.

After you have demonstrated for yourself that these intuitive abilities are indeed available, you may begin to wonder about other aspects of the nonlocal mind. The true value of remote viewing lies in the fact that it puts us in contact with the part of our consciousness that is clearly unbounded by distance or time. Remote viewing allows us to become aware of our connected, interdependent nature.

Furthermore, we now know that it is no more difficult to experience the future than it is to perceive the hidden present. In the following chapter, we will explore precognition — remote viewing of the future.

CHAPTER FOUR

precognition

THERE'S NO TIME LIKE THE FUTURE
— OR THE PAST

*Quantum theory indicates that there are no such things
as separate parts in reality, but instead only intimately related
phenomena so bound up with each other as to be inseparable.*

— Professor Henry Stapp

Our ability to expand our personal awareness through time as well
as space provides the strongest possible evidence for our timeless
existence. Our peaceful mind can learn to reside outside of time,
in a place free of depression about the past, anxiety about the
future, or fear of the present. This spacious state of timelessness
manifests as the quiet mind. Our ability to move our awareness
deliberately through time and space offers powerful, life-changing
experiences, demonstrating clearly that we are not merely bodies
but, rather, timeless awareness residing as a body.

If you have carried out some of the exercises in the previous chapter, you now know from your own experience that there is no separation in consciousness, as the mystics have been telling us over the millennia. Mystics will never ask you to take what they say as a matter of faith; the mystic dwells in the world of experience. When Joseph Campbell, the great expert on mythology and world religions, was interviewed by Bill Moyers on their television series *The Power of Myth,* Moyers asked Campbell if he was a man of "great faith." A man of many travels and much study, Campbell replied, "I don't need faith; I have experience."

I, too, have been blessed with a wide range of personal psychic experiences. These have shown me, in striking ways, the freedom we have to travel not only forward in time, but backward as well. In this chapter, I will describe some of my own experiences in this arena, together with the best time-traveling data from laboratory research.

DREAMS OF THE FUTURE

Precognitive dreams are probably the most common psychic occurrence in the life of the average person. These dreams often give us a glimpse of events that we will experience the next day or in the near future. In fact, I believe that the precognitive dream may be caused by the experience that we have at that future time. For example, if you have a dream of an elephant passing in front of your window, and you wake up the next morning to find a circus parade led by an elephant going down your street, I would say that the previous night's dream of an elephant was caused by your experience of seeing the elephant the next morning. This is an example of the future affecting the past — which isn't as strange as it sounds when you realize that we are all timeless awareness.

There is an enormous body of evidence to support this model

of causality. What cannot happen, however, is a future event changing the past. Nothing in the future can cause something that has
already happened to not have happened. This is called the "intervention paradox." This paradox is illustrated by the well-known
thought experiment in which a man psychically kills his grandmother in the past, when she was a child, thereby preventing
himself from ever coming into existence. This kind of thing is interesting to think about, but there is not a drop of evidence to make
us take it seriously. There are some things you simply can't do!

To know that a dream is precognitive, you must recognize that
it is not caused by the previous day's mental residue, by your
wishes, or by anxieties. Precognitive dreams have an unusual clarity, and they often contain bizarre or unfamiliar material. Dream
experts like to speak of the preternatural (uncanny) clarity of
precognitive dreams. These are not wish-fulfillment or anxiety
dreams. For example, if you are unprepared for an exam and you
dream about failing it, we would not consider this to be precognition but ordinary cause and effect. On the other hand, if you have
taken hundreds of plane flights over many years without anxiety,
then have a frightening dream about a crash, you might want to
rethink your travel plans. During the SRI remote-viewing program, our CIA contract monitor saved his own life by delaying his
flight out of Detroit after a particularly frightening dream about
being in a plane crash. Unfortunately, his partner did take the
flight. As another example of this phenomenon, on the day after
the 9/11 tragedy I read in the *International Herald Tribune* that
there were many fewer passengers on each of the four crashed
planes than would normally be traveling at that hour.

One of the most interesting questions in all of psychical
research pertains to how we might make use of precognition in
our lives. Might you be able to use precognitive information to
change a future that you perceive but do not like? A problem arises

when we try to answer this; if you change the future so that the unpleasant thing doesn't happen to you, where did the dream come from?

First of all, a precognitive dream is not a prophecy; it is a forecast, based on all presently available "world lines" (possible paths through space and time; see Chapter 1). If I wish to make use of my newly received, precognitively derived information, I believe I can change the future. For example, I might have a frightening dream about being in a car crash and dying. If the dream is especially vivid, I might want to take my car to the mechanic and ask him to look it over. If his inspection reveals that all but one of the nuts has fallen off one of the car's wheels, his inspection, inspired by my worrisome dream, may have prevented the crash and saved my life. (Needless to say, I prefer this outcome to the one in the dream.) This new result does not falsify my initial forecast. Bertrand Russell describes this supposed vicious-circle paradox in his writing on Theory of Types:[1]

> A dream is only a forecast of events to come about in the future unless you do something to change them based upon the information in the dream. Such an action does not falsify the forecast. There is no paradox. In this case it is a dream about a probable future that does not become actualized.

Another question might be, "How can I dream about being in a plane crash or a collision, then later find out that just such an event occurred, but without me in it?" The answer here is quite different. You dream about the real crash, in which you do not take part, and then dramatize the events in your dream to include yourself in it. We would say that the frightening crash that actually occurs can be the stimulus or cause of a dream the previous night. This is called *retrocausality*, and it may be the basis of most precognition.

A Typical Precognitive Dream

I have a strong visual sense, and I often have memorable dreams. Several years ago, I had a striking dream while attending a scientific conference where I was to present a technical paper. I dreamed that the person who was going to speak before me was standing at the lectern, dressed in a tuxedo with a red carnation in his lapel, and that he was going to sing his paper. This dream, unlike many that I have, certainly did not reflect any wish-fulfillment or residue of the previous day's experience, and it had the unique clarity and bizarre nature that I have come to associate with precognitive dreams. The next morning, I told Hal Puthoff about my dream. On our way to breakfast, we went to the hotel meeting room to see what it looked like. At the lectern, beyond the rows of chairs, stood a man in a tuxedo wearing a red carnation in his lapel. I went up to him and asked if he was going to sing. "Yes," he said, "but not until later." He turned out to be a bandleader who would be using the conference room later in the day for a banquet at which he planned to sing! It was my analytical mind that made him into a colleague presenting a paper.

DREAMING OF THE PAST

During my last trip to Italy, where I was to teach with Jane Katra, I had a surprising *retrocognitive* dream (a dream about past events of which I was unaware). In this dream, I was at a religious ashram that looked to me like a summer camp. As I was walking up to an outdoor table in this dry, dusty landscape, a short woman with curly, dark hair came up to me and excitedly invited me to see films of her "guru." I agreed, but said that I wanted to eat first. The dark-haired woman then picked up something that looked like pink Japanese ginger from a trestle table, and she offered to feed it to me. I accepted it, and began to choke because it tasted like carpet sweepings. I continued to choke until I awakened. That was the dream.

The next morning, I related this strange dream to Jane. I'd recently had two dreams about things we would see in Milan, which we then actually saw, and I wanted to get credit for yet another precognitive dream. (No ego here; this was just science.) Jane then told me she'd had essentially the experience I described the previous day: While I was on the stage of our lecture room setting up a slide projector on its trestle table, Jane, in the far reaches of the auditorium, had been accosted by a short, dark-haired woman who was one of our students. This woman wanted to show Jane some pictures of her guru, Sai Baba. The pictures were interesting because they showed the famous guru at a peace conference in Assisi, even though he was never physically in attendance (we were told). The woman then excitedly opened her purse and took out a little white box filled with orange powder. She took a pinch and popped it into Jane's open mouth, at which point Jane launched into a fit of coughing. She was told that the powder was sacred *vibuti* that had been magically produced by Sai Baba at a meeting the previous year. My dream that night was a surprisingly accurate recapitulation of Jane's experience the previous day, of which I'd been completely ignorant.

Jane and I have shared many such timeless interchanges in which I experienced her physical state or condition. Early in our work together, Jane suggested that I "look in on her" at 10:00 P.M. one night at her home in Eugene, Oregon. At the appointed time, I dimmed the lights, sat cross-legged (not a remote-viewing requirement) on my bed in Palo Alto, California, and focused my attention on my new friend, Jane. I visualized myself going north to her house, a technique Bob Monroe describes in his book, *Journeys Out of the Body*.[2] I "saw" her carrying a silver tray in a dimly lit room. I had the feeling that she was offering me a piece of cake. As I was about to accept it, the whole plate was pushed into my face, and I fell over backward on my bed. Can you guess what was actually going on up in Eugene? It turned out that Jane had entirely forgotten about our experiment and was watching videos with her family. Close to 10:00 P.M., she decided to make popcorn. She poured the hot, fragrant popcorn into a large stainless-steel mixing bowl. At the exact time of our experiment, Jane, as many of us have done, put her face into the bowl to snag pieces of popcorn with her tongue. That was the source of my "silver-plate-in-the-face" experience. I would attribute the similarities between what Jane was doing and what I "saw" to ESP, and the differences to various kinds of mental noise.

Jane and I have now written, worked, and taught together for a decade. From time to time, my internal visions and feelings pertaining to her distant activities are so accurate, profound, and vivid that they take on the appearance of "quantum entanglement born of a singular wave function." In this phenomenon, two photons are created together and travel away from each other at the speed of light. Despite their separation, anything that happens to one of them affects the other.

I have learned, and believe without the slightest doubt, that as one surrenders more and more to the remote-viewing experience, many things will occur other than seeing pictures on one's mental screen. I believe that, in the remote-viewing practice, we are given brief glimpses of timeless existence. In contemporary terms, I would say that if we live in a nonlocal universe, as we appear to, then we are, or can be, in direct contact with both our past and future selves. The contact is there, and we get to choose whether we will be aware of it. Erwin Schrödinger was so impressed with the importance of quantum entanglement and nonlocality that he wrote about it in his seminal 1935 paper (in which he introduced his celebrated paradox of the cat that was quantum-mechanically neither alive nor dead):

[Entanglement is] not one, but rather the, characteristic trait of quantum mechanics — the *one* that enforces its entire departure from classical lines of thought.[3]

THE PARANORMAL FUTURE

There is much more to precognition than my personal experiences. In a summary of research data from 1935 to 1987 on what we call "paranormal foreknowledge of the future," my good friends Charles Honorton and Diane Ferrari examined reports of 309 precognition experiments that had been carried out by sixty-two investigators.[4] More than 50,000 participants were involved in more than 2 million trials. Thirty percent of these studies were statistically significant in showing that people can describe future events, whereas only 5 percent would be expected to be able to do this by chance — a sixfold increase. Because of the large number of trials, this gave overall significance of greater than 10^{20} to 1, which is akin to throwing seventy pennies in the air and having every one come down heads-up. This body of data offers strong evidence confirming the existence of foreknowledge of the future. Based on my own work, I have no doubt that we have contact with the future; this shows unequivocally that we misunderstand our relationship to the dimension of time that we take so much for granted.

HOW DOES PRECOGNITION AFFECT THE BODY?

How can we make use of this slipperiness we experience as we slide up and down the dimension of time? Based on both my personal experiences and the research with mental time-travel, I believe that we can derive information from the future. I have described how, in dreams, the future appears to influence the present. Could we then, by an act of our own will, affect the past (recognizing, of course, that we cannot change it)? Furthermore, can we learn to heal an illness that has now become serious — in its earlier stages when it did not yet appear life-threatening? Can we send healing thoughts into someone's past to help them be less sick than they presently are?

Researcher William Braud and many others think that this is a possibility worth investigating.[5] Surprisingly, there are data suggesting that we can facilitate this healing — as long as no one knows how sick the patient really is. According to the "observational theory" of psi, an early and definitive diagnosis of an illness might serve to "lock in" the illness, thereby making it impossible to affect or cure it retrocausally. But if you go to a healer when you are suffering from vague, undiagnosed complaints, she might be able to reach into your past and send you healing information that you can incorporate into your physiology in a health-promoting way.

There are two groups of laboratory data that support this remarkable assertion. I will describe them in the next section, but first I want to introduce you to a concept that will help you understand these studies better. We are all familiar with the idea of a premonition, in which one has inner knowledge of something that is going to happen in the future — usually something bad! There is also an experience called *presentiment,* in which one has an inner sensation — a gut feeling that something strange is about to occur. An example: You suddenly stop on your walk down the street because you feel "uneasy," only to have a flowerpot fall off a window ledge and land at your feet, instead of on your head. This would be a useful presentiment.

I have had such a useful presentiment. One Friday evening, I was quietly paying bills at my desk when I began to worry obsessively about what would happen if I lost my credit card. (I had never previously lost a credit card.) This fear was so strong that I stopped what I was doing, went into the next room to get my credit card from my wallet, and compulsively wrote its numbers in my personal telephone book. The next day I went to a big street fair that covered many blocks of University Avenue, the main street of Palo Alto. While there, I bought some beautiful blue ceramic bowls. It was a very hot day, and a concessionaire was selling cold beer and celebratory beer mugs. Alas, I had just spent all my cash. I went to an ATM at a nearby bank and obtained some beer money. Now, with cash in one hand and a long colorful receipt in the other hand, I set off to get my treat to deal with the heat. Two days later, while trying to pay for my groceries, I discovered with a shock that my credit card was missing from my wallet. After some thought, I deduced that I had probably left it in the ATM at the street fair. Because of my presentiment, I had the card numbers written down and was able to call the credit card company and ask for a new card. That's one reward for paying attention to presentiments!

Physical Responses

In the laboratory, we know that if we show a frightening picture to a person, there will be a significant change in his or her physiology. Blood pressure, heart rate, and skin resistance will all change. This fight-or-flight reaction is called an "orienting response." Researcher Dean Radin at the University of Nevada (now at the Institute of Noetic Sciences) has shown that this orienting response is also observed in a person's physiology a few seconds before they see the scary picture.[6] In balanced double-blind experiments, Radin has demonstrated that if experimental subjects are about to see scenes of sexuality, violence, or mayhem, their bodies will steel themselves against the surprise, shock, or insult. But if the subjects are about to see a picture of a flower garden, there is no such strong anticipatory reaction — even before the picture is randomly selected! Fear is much easier to measure physiologically than bliss.

The pictures that Radin uses in his experiments are from a standardized, quantified set of emotional stimuli used in psychology research. These range from nudes on the beach and downhill skiing on the positive side, to car crashes and abdominal surgery

— generally considered to have a negative effect. In the neutral range are pictures of paper cups and fountain pens. Perhaps Radin's most exciting result is that the more emotional the picture shown to the subject, the greater the magnitude of the subject's "prestimulus response." Radin reports this correlation to be significant at odds greater than 100 to 1. Professor Dick Bierman at Utrecht University in Holland has successfully replicated Radin's findings, but he had to assemble a much more "extreme" set of pictures in order to psychically excite his more worldly Amsterdam college students.

I would say that these experiments describe the case in which one's direct physical perception of a picture, when it occurs, causes one to have a unique physical response at an earlier time; one's future is affecting one's past. William Braud, in his excellent new book, *Distant Mental Influence*, describes these experiments as follows:

> Although this presentiment effect is usually taken to reflect precognition (future-knowing) operating at an unconscious body level, these interesting findings can just as well be interpreted as instances in which objective events (the presentation of the slide itself or the person's future reaction to the slide) may be acting backward in time to influence the person's physiology.7

Even stronger results have been obtained by physicists Edwin May and James Spottiswoode, who measured the galvanic skin response of subjects who were about to hear a loud noise from time to time through earphones. Again, measurements from more than one hundred participants showed that their nervous systems seemed to know three to five seconds in advance when it would be assaulted with a disagreeable stimulus. It is as though our physiological "now" has a three-second temporal span.

The most significant evidence for this prestimulus response comes from the Hungarian researcher Zoltán Vassy. Vassy administered painful electric shocks as the stimulus to be precognized. His results are the strongest of all because the human body does not habituate to electric shocks. To illustrate this point: When I was a subject in Edwin May's experiment, after I heard a few loud-noise stimuli my body realized that the noise wasn't going to hurt me; I became more meditative than vigilant, causing a decline in the prestimulus response. But an electric shock is always experienced as a new and alarming stimulus, even though it resides in one's future.[8]

Experiments with a similar interpretation were carried out by Helmut Schmidt at the Mind Science Foundation in Austin, Texas. Schmidt was examining the behavior of electronic random-number generators that produce long, haphazard strings of ones and zeros.[9] The source of randomness in these experiments is radioactive decay: Electrons from radioactive material cause random pulses to be generated by a Geiger counter. Modern physics considers this quantum mechanical process to be utterly unpredictable and uncontrollable. Yet the body of work Schmidt had already amassed showed that a person could mentally interact with the random-number-generating machine from a distance — that is, to obtain more ones or zeros just by paying attention to the desired outcome while the machine was running.

In his latest and most remarkable experiments, Schmidt has shown that, even after the machine has completed its run and has generated a tape recording of its output of ones and zeros, a person can still affect the outcome by paying attention to the tape — as long as no one has seen the data beforehand. We do not believe that the person is actually changing the original data (often a punched-hole paper tape). Rather, Schmidt and others believe that the person who is listening to the tape at a later time is reaching back to an earlier time to affect the machine at the time of its operation.

Schmidt has even demonstrated that the prerecorded, but unobserved, breathing rate of laboratory volunteers from an earlier day can be affected (made faster or slower) by the mental activity of a person listening to the recording at a later time![10]

Both of these experiments suggest that a healer can, similarly, reach back in time far enough to affect her patient's (or even her own) physiology at an early decision point, when a healing outcome can still be achieved. Taking cognizance of the nonlocal nature of our universe, William Braud has recently conjectured in a paper in *Alternative Therapies in Health and Medicine* that our healing intentions may achieve their goal by reaching backward in time to affect the critical "seed moments" in alternate future pathways of the development of the illness. Braud suggests that these early moments may be more labile, and hence more susceptible, avenues of change in distant healing.[11]

This idea of backward causation is like the previously described experience of precognitive dreams, in which one's dream in the night is ostensibly "caused" by the confirmatory experience, which one typically has the next day. Modern physics seems to indicate that we live in a spiderweb of space and time, in which both the future and the past are tugging on the present. We do not yet know what kind of physiology is most amenable to such treatment, or how far into the past the healer can reach; these are exciting questions that remain to be answered. I will further explore distant healing and related concepts in Chapter 6.

ASSOCIATIVE REMOTE VIEWING

As I mentioned in Chapter 2, in 1982 I was part of a team of psychics and investors who wanted to see if it was possible to use psychic functioning to make money in the marketplace. The team consisted of an experienced remote viewer, an enthusiastic investor, a businessman, an adventurous stockbroker, and me as interviewer. We called ourselves Delphi Associates. It is well understood that reading numbers or letters psychically is an exceptionally difficult task. So we couldn't forecast silver commodity prices by asking our psychic to read the symbols on the big board at the New York Commodity Exchange a week in the future. Instead, we used a protocol first described by psychical researcher and archaeologist Stephen Schwartz.

In this scheme, we associated a different object with each of the possible states the silver market could be in during the following week. We wanted to know a week in advance whether the commodity called "December silver" would be "up a little" (less than a quarter or unchanged), "up a lot" (more than a quarter), "down a little," or "down a lot." These are four discrete conditions that could, for example, be represented by a light bulb, a flower, a book, a rock, or a stuffed animal. For the first week's trial, we asked our businessman to choose four such strongly differing objects and associate them with each of our four possible conditions. Only he knew the objects. I then interviewed the remote viewer over the telephone and asked him to describe his impressions of the object we would show him the following week. The broker then bought or sold silver futures contracts based entirely on what the viewer saw, whether it be a flower, a teddy bear, or whatever. This would be the object associated with what the market would do in the next week, which is why we call this "associative" remote viewing. At the end of the week, when silver finally closed, we liquidated our position and showed the viewer the object that corresponded to what the market actually did. Our nine forecasts in the fall of 1982 were all correct, and we earned over $100,000, which we divided with our investor. We were on the front page of the *Wall Street Journal,* and *NOVA* made a film about us called "A Case of ESP."[12]

The following year we were not as successful. Our investor wanted to carry out two trials per week, which significantly confused and rushed our protocol — especially the critically important feedback to the viewer. I believe that we also lost our "spiritual focus" which, in that the first series, was at least partially for science. In the second series, we were definitely out to break the bank; serious greed had entered into our planning. Each of the participants has his own idea about why we could not repeat our initial stunning success.

Since then, Jane Katra and I have personally conducted many experimental series in which people have described and experienced events that didn't occur until two or three days in the future. One of these we carried out in the living room of my house in 1995, with the help of two friends. This series, performed at the suggestion of our publisher, was a formal precognitive experiment to forecast changes in the silver commodity market (up or down), in which we were successful in eleven out of twelve individual calls.[13] This was again associative remote viewing with small objects to be revealed at a later time, although no money was involved in this experiment. We, therefore, have no doubt that the precognitive channel is available to almost anyone.

We know from the experimental data of psi research that a viewer in the laboratory can focus his or her attention anywhere on the planet and, about two-thirds of the time, describe what is there. We also know that this same viewer is not bound by present time. As I said earlier, in contemporary physics, we call this ability to focus attention on distant points in space-time "nonlocal" awareness. Based on the accumulated data of the past thirty years, I believe that an experienced viewer can answer any question that has an answer — about events in the past, present, or future.

Physicist David Bohm says that we greatly misunderstand the illusion of separation in space and time. In his physics textbook, *The Undivided Universe,* he tries to defuse this illusion as he writes about the quantum-interconnectedness of all things.[14] As Norman Friedman puts it, "It is as though events do not occur [in time], they just are."[15] Emerson and Thoreau, as well as many Transcendentalists after them, have called this interconnectedness an *oversoul,* or a community of spirit. From what we have already related, it should be apparent that our personal connection to this nonlocal spiritual community has many of the omnipresent and omniscient properties that people often associate with an experience of God.

PRECOGNITION IN THE LAB

Religious convictions notwithstanding, parapsychologists have for years been trying to find ways to encourage their subjects to demonstrate psychic glimpses of the future. Earlier in this chapter, I mentioned a large retrospective analysis by Charles Honorton and Diane Ferrari, of 309 precognition experiments carried out over the fifty years between 1935 and 1987. These were forced-choice experiments, in which subjects had to choose which of four colored buttons would be illuminated right after their choice, or which of five cards they would be shown at a later time. In all of these cases, a random-number generator of some sort selected the targets, to which the researchers were "blind." Participants had to guess what they would be shown in the future, from among known alternatives. In some cases, they had to choose which target would be randomly chosen in the future, with no feedback at all as to which turned out to be the correct target.

There are two kinds of important information for us in this study. We see that there is overwhelming evidence for the existence of precognition but, more important, we learn that there are more successful and less successful ways to do experiments. Four factors were found to correlate significantly with success or failure in these experiments. It is important to keep the following factors in mind if you want your own experiments to succeed.

Experiments are much more successful when they are carried out with subjects who are experienced and interested in the outcome, rather than people who are inexperienced and uninterested. For example, running ESP experiments using a whole classroom of moderately bored students will rarely show any kind of success. Participants who are enthusiastic about the experiment are the most successful in these precognition studies. The difference in scoring rate between these two kinds of tests — using experienced and inexperienced subjects — was significant at 1,000 to 1 against chance.

Tests that used individual subjects were much more successful than experiments with groups. Additionally, making the trials meaningful to each participant was important to success. The success level comparing individuals to groups was statistically significant at 30 to 1 against chance.

I have always felt that feedback is one of the most helpful channels in all psi functioning. In precognition, we've found that the viewer's experience when shown the target at a later time is often the source of the precognitive perception. Nonetheless, studies by Gertrude Schmeidler at City College of New York showed significant precognition with college students in forced-choice trials of computer-generated targets, even when the viewers did not receive any feedback.[16]

At a week-long workshop of ESP researchers, Elisabeth Targ and I carried out a formal study at the beautiful Esalen Institute in Big Sur, California, to examine the feedback question. In a balanced experiment, two by-then experienced viewers, Hella Hammid and Marilyn Schlitz, were asked to describe the picture that was being shown on the wall in the next room. Half the time they were allowed to see the target picture after the trial. Statistically significant remote viewing was present even in the case without feedback. The judges for these twelve trials were also blind as to which picture was shown in a given session, so we conclude that feedback is helpful but not critical, especially for experienced viewers.[17]

Finally, the data show that the sooner the participants get their feedback, the greater the hit rate. That is, it appears that for forced-choice targets, it is easier to foretell the immediate future than the distant future. In laboratory experiments, people did very well in predicting events seconds or minutes in advance, but did less well looking hours or days into the future. This seems to be the case for naturally occurring precognition (such as dreams) as well. On the other hand, it is also possible that people tend to forget dreams of far-future events before they have a chance to be corroborated.

Thus, the four factors that are important in these studies are:

1. Practiced vs. inexperienced subjects
2. Individual vs. group testing
3. Feedback vs. no feedback
4. Short time interval between target generation and subject response

In the whole database of the Honorton-Ferrari analysis, some experiments had all four favorable factors, and some had all four unfavorable factors. After all is said and done, 87.5 percent of the most psi-conducive studies were successful and significant, while none of the studies done under all unfavorable conditions were statistically significant. Since we now routinely carry out experiments under the favorable conditions, I think we can say that we have learned something about psi in the past fifty years.

Actually, we have learned quite a lot. We know, for example, that forced-choice ESP tests are an inefficient way to elicit psi functioning; they always have an additional burden of boredom and mental noise (AOL). In the above studies, the experimenters, on average, had to carry out 3,600 trials to achieve a statistically significant result. With the free-response type of experiment, such as remote viewing, we typically have to do only six to nine trials.

As I mentioned in Chapter 1, researchers Robert Jahn and Brenda Dunne at Princeton University carried out a total of 411 published remote-viewing trials over a twenty-five-year period.[18] They showed conclusively that remote-viewing accuracy and reliability do not decline with increasing distance from the viewer, nor with increasing time into the future — an important contribution. They also found that their success rate declined over the years, as they and the experimenters and viewers paid increasing attention to scoring and analytical evaluation and check-off schemes, and decreasing attention to the viewers' process and their feedback. (There is more on the Princeton work later in this section.) There was no such decline in the even more voluminous SRI database extending over the same time period.

In an imaginative series of experiments in the 1970s involving precognitive dreams, Stanley Krippner, Montague Ullman, and Charles Honorton found that only eight trials were needed to show the effects of precognition.[19] These researchers at the Maimonides Dream Laboratory in Brooklyn, New York, worked with Malcolm Besant, a successful English psychic (possibly related to Annie Besant, one of the founders of the Theosophical Society). In two formal series of eight trials each, Malcolm was asked to dream in the laboratory about the events that he would experience the next morning. Several dozen of these possible next-day experiences had previously been devised by the creative laboratory staff and written down on file cards. After going to sleep, Malcolm was awakened from time to time during the night when his EEG showed by the appearance of rapid eye movements (REM sleep) that he was dreaming. His dream reports were all tape-recorded. The next morning, other lab staff used a random-number generator to choose one of the experience cards. Malcolm was then led through that experience. In one typical case, Malcolm dreamed of being in a cold, white room with small blue objects while experiencing the feeling of being very chilled. When he awakened, the experimenters took him into another room, where they dropped ice cubes down his shirt while two blue electric fans blew cold air on him. It certainly sounds as if the morning's ice cubes were the cause of his chilly dream the previous night.

In my experiments with Hal Puthoff at SRI, the first case of precognition appeared spontaneously during a session in 1974. I was sitting with Pat Price in our little shielded room on the second floor of the Radio Physics building, about to start one of the trials in the formal series described in Chapter 2. I had described who we were and what we were doing for the tape recorder, and Pat and I were chatting about the experiment in progress. Our lab director, Bart Cox, was the target selector for this trial because he wanted to have the experiment under his complete personal control. He decided to drive out of SRI and turn his car randomly at intersections until he decided that he was at an acceptable target location. Hal was with Bart on this random drive. Meanwhile, Pat was explaining to me that we didn't have to wait for Bart to actually choose a target; Pat could just look "down the time line" and see where Bart and Hal would wind up in half an hour! Pat's description on the tape was:

> What I am looking at is a little boat jetty, or a little boat dock along the bay — in a direction like that from here (he pointed in the correct direction). Yeah, I see little boats, some motor launches, some little sailing ships, sails all furled, some with their masts stepped, others are up. Little jetty, or a dock there. Funny thing — this just flashed in —

kind of looks like a Chinese or Japanese pagoda effect. It's a definite feeling of Oriental architecture that seems to be fairly adjacent to where they are.[20]

Pat completed his description fifteen minutes before the travelers arrived at their site. A half-hour later, Bart and Hal returned to SRI to see what Pat had to say. It turned out that we all had plenty to say because they had found their way to the Redwood City Marina. The marina is a harbor and boat dock about four miles north of SRI. It is full of small- and medium-sized sailboats, and it is right next to a restaurant with a curved sloping roof that looks very Asian indeed. Pat had a full precognitive experience of the marina, including a discussion of how much he liked the smell of the sea air, all before the target was even chosen!

The next year, in 1975, we conducted a series of four deliberately precognitive trials with Hella Hammid. Like the experiments with Pat Price, each trial involved a pair of people traveling to an undetermined place, which Hella described before they arrived there. Each of her four remote-viewing descriptions was correctly matched in first place to its respective target — a significant departure from chance expectation.[21] One of these trials was especially striking for me. I still remember sitting with her as she described a location with "manicured trees and shrubs, and a formal garden." She went on to describe a path leading to a balcony and steps. After the travelers returned from their target location, Hella and I joined them for feedback on a return visit to their site. It was an extraordinary déjà vu experience to listen to Hella's tape-recorded description of the Stanford University Hospital gardens as we walked through them.

Einstein believed in a four-dimensional "block universe" of relativistic space and time, in which we follow a world line — the time line of our life — that is already frozen in place. That is to say, the future is not chosen, it just appears — without choice, and predetermined in our awareness. The eminent French physicist Olivier Costa de Beauregard, who happens to be deeply interested

in psi phenomena, has written about our deterministic creeping
along this time line. He writes:

> Humans and other living creatures... are compelled to
> explore, little by little, the content of the fourth dimension,
> as each one traverses, without stopping or turning back, a
> time-like trajectory in space-time.[22]

The equally eminent Neils Bohr has a more optimistic view.
His picture is that we are neither free nor not free. In his comple-
mentary approach to quantum mechanics, he is quoted by de
Beauregard as saying:

> Just as freedom of will is an experiential category of our
> psychic life, causality may be called a mode of perception,
> by which we reduce our sense perceptions to order.[23]

I believe that precognitive perception plays an active role in
our ability to make choices, both consciously and unconsciously.
Informed by our psychic knowledge of the future, it allows us to
leave the fatalistic plane of mechanical determinism by providing
the information to make us free.

One of the recurring questions in precognition research con-
cerns the source of the mental images that the viewer experiences.
Do the images come directly from the target or from the future
feedback? A clear example of this kind of phenomenon is
described in the wonderful book *An Experiment with Time*, by
English engineer J. W. Dunne.[24] Dunne's book, first published in
1927, is a treasure trove of precognition data. In one of many
examples of his precognitive dreams, he reports having had a clear
impression of a volcanic eruption in which 4,000 people were
killed. The next morning, he read in the newspaper of that very
event, including a report of 4,000 fatalities. It wasn't until he prepared his book for publication, and looked again at the article,
that he discovered that it actually referred to 40,000 deaths, not

the 4,000 he had thought he read of in the newspaper. As it turned out, the number of lives lost in the eruption was different from both these numbers; his dream of a specific number apparently came from his precognition of misreading of the paper.

As noted earlier in this chapter, the most comprehensive laboratory examination of precognition was done by Robert Jahn, Brenda Dunne, and Roger Nelson at Princeton University.[25] They conducted 227 formal experiments in which a viewer was asked to

© The *New Yorker* Collection 1979 J. B. Handelsman from cartoonbank.com. All Rights Reserved.

describe where one of the researchers would be hiding at some pre-
selected later time — around Princeton, or across the country.
They discovered, much to their surprise, that the accuracy of the
description was the same whether the viewer had to look hours or
days into the future. The statistical significance of the combined
experiments departed from chance by a probability of 10^{-11}, or one
in a hundred billion! Their findings are so strong that it is hard to
read about their work and not be convinced of the reality of precognition, even though we don't understand how it works.

BACK TO THE FUTURE

One of my great passions over the years has been pursuing the
issues of precognition and probable futures. The most important
outstanding question is whether a remote viewer sees the actual
future or the probable future. That is, does the viewer see what is
likely to happen, or what actually occurs? Elisabeth Targ and I carried out an experiment to investigate this question.[26]

Elisabeth designed an ingenious experiment with twelve precognitive trials. For each trial, there was a pool of six possible
target objects, to be chosen among by a 0-to-9 electronic random-
number generator. One particular object would be the target if the
generator came up with any number from 0 to 4, so that object
had a 50-percent chance of being chosen. Each of the other five
objects would be chosen if its number — 5, 6, 7, 8, or 9 — came
up. Thus, each of these latter five objects had a one-in-ten probability of being chosen. The viewer's task, as always, was to describe
the object that would be revealed at the end of each trial. The
question posed by the experiment was whether the presence of a
50-percent-probable target would interfere with the viewer's ability to correctly describe a 10-percent-probable object when it was
chosen by the random-number generator. We found that there

was no such interference. The viewers saw the actualized and chosen future, not the probable future. Thus, from a psychic point of view, what you see is what you're going to get (unless you alter it by using your psychic data).

An example of such a probable future comes from an applied remote-viewing task that we performed in 1976. One of our government customers asked us to psychically describe what would be occurring at a particular set of geographical coordinates (latitude and longitude) four days in the future. Ingo Swann was the viewer. He said that he saw a very colorful scene, and asked us to get his colored pencils so that he could color in his sketch. What he drew looked to us like a great multicolored fountain. He said it was some sort of pyrotechnic display. The actual target, we learned three weeks later, was a forthcoming Chinese atomic bomb test. What could be discerned from Ingo's drawing at the time by an intelligence expert was that the test probably failed (or would fail). This was apparent because burning uranium creates not an explosion, but a pyrotechnic fountain of colored fire and sparks. Today's question is: Could the Chinese have fixed the problem in advance if we had given them Ingo's precognitive information before their test? Was Ingo seeing the probable future, or the actual future?

WHAT DOES IT MEAN TO BE TIMELESS?

We now know that our timeless awareness has mobility independent of our physical body. The evidence is very strong that awareness, which is what we are, can receive an inflow of information from all of space-time, and can generate an outflow of healing intention to the present, the future, and the past. This all happens because space-time is nonlocal and there is no separation in consciousness. The Hindu Vedas, written even before the time of Buddha, teach that consciousness is the ground of all being. That is, consciousness predates, and is independent of, life as we know it.

The nineteenth-century English scholar F. W. H. Myers spent a good part of his life investigating mediumistic evidence for survival of human personality after death of the body. His great book, *Human Personality and Its Survival of Bodily Death*,[27] gives many examples of spirit communications that sound surprisingly like long-distance telephone calls from the dead. Nonetheless, he felt that the only way one could be certain that a spiritual communication came directly from a previously alive person's spirit or surviving awareness, rather than via the medium's clairvoyance of present-time information, would be for the spirit to communicate information that the medium could not know, even psychically.

After Myers died, he carried out this experiment posthumously: The deceased Myers apparently sent independent fragmentary messages to three well-known and widely separated mediums — in England, India, and the United States. The messages made sense only when they were combined and analyzed at the Society for Psychical Research in London. These celebrated communications are known as the "cross-correspondence cases." They are like three meaningless pieces of a jigsaw puzzle that show a recognizable picture only when they are all put together. Many of these complex transmissions were drawn from Myers's knowledge of classical Greek and Roman plays and poetry. A detailed and thoughtful examination of the cross-correspondence cases is presented by Harold Francis Saltmarsh in his book, *The Future and Beyond*.[28]

Another aspect of these communications that interested Myers was *xenoglossy,* wherein the medium brings a message from a dead person and speaks it in a foreign language to which the medium has never been exposed. I experienced such a case one week after my daughter Elisabeth died, in 2002, when her husband Mark received a letter from a woman in Seattle. The Seattle woman was one of the spiritual healers who participated in Elisabeth's successful experiment on distant prayer. In the woman's dream, which occurred a few days after Elisabeth's death, Elisabeth came to her with an urgent message for Mark, but the woman could not understand it at all. She thought the message was nonsense syllables. Elisabeth kept repeating them over and over, then woke the woman up so that she could write them down phonetically.

When Mark opened the letter, he saw the message: two rows of English letters, with each row arranged in four three-letter groups — like a code. As he tried to read the message, I recognized the first group of syllables as the Russian words for "I love you." I didn't recognize the second group, but a native Russian speaker has since told us that they say "I adore you" in idiomatic Russian. The Seattle lady claims not to know Russian, nor has she ever to her knowledge been exposed to it or any language other than English. Elisabeth was a translator and, of course, was fluent in Russian. We believe this is just the sort of message Elisabeth would send to establish that she is still present somewhere.

The following night, three of us were sitting on the deck outside my house, looking out across San Francisco Bay and watching the airplanes fly past the crescent moon on their way to the airport. The house was dark, but I'd left the lights on in the foyer. As we discussed the previous day's mysterious letter, the foyer lights in the nearly darkened house flashed dramatically off, then on again. Since these were the only lights that had been on, this was very noticeable to us all. As we wondered aloud if it could be a signal from Elisabeth, the lights then flashed off and on two more times. We were sitting just outside the room in which Elisabeth had passed away the previous week, and we were all silenced and overcome with awe. There was no known electrical problem, and I like to believe that she is still trying to keep us in touch with the truth, much as Myers did a century earlier. Psychiatrist Daniel Benor reports that more than two-thirds of all people have had the experience of seeing an apparition of a deceased loved one.[29]

In Chapter 5, I will venture into intuitive medical diagnosis — a more analytical aspect of remote viewing, but intuitive nevertheless. For some, like myself, this process is even easier than remote viewing of a nonliving system. Researchers have been writing books about this subject since the 1950s; now we know a bit more about how and why it works.

intuitive medical

diagnosis

THINGS TO DO BEFORE THE DOCTOR ARRIVES

Intuitive medical diagnosis is more analytical and less intuitive than most distant healing, but it is still intuitive. For example, a spiritual healer doesn't need to know, and often doesn't want to know, the nature of the illness suffered by her distant patient. The spiritual healer is interested in relieving pain and achieving coherence and wholeness — as though providing a healing template for wellness. This is a kind of Platonic model in which the healer supports the body's homeostasis for immune-system equilibrium. In order to be truly helpful, however, a person doing psychic diagnosis must be able to identify and name the body system that is out of balance. An intuitive diagnostician should also be able to identify the underlying physical and psychological causes for the problem — whether they be stress, injury, or a forgotten trauma.

EVEN A SCIENTIST CAN DO IT

In Chapter 2, I emphasized the point that analytical functions, such as naming, are the part of a psychic description least likely to be correct. This is true for an object in a bag or a box, but it doesn't appear to be true in intuitive diagnosis. It appears that if you know the names of the bodily systems, you will be better able to identify them in a medical reading.

In the 1970s, two popular training programs — Silva Mind Control and Erhard Seminars Training (EST) — had all their students perform intuitive readings as part of their graduation exercises. The participants were required to relate the physical characteristics and behavior of an unknown person described on a file card in an envelope held by another student or graduate. Even the most resistant students were able to do this surprisingly well.

I am a successful teacher of remote viewing and a moderately skilled viewer (although not as good as the psychic superstars described earlier). In the past year, I have been exploring intuitive diagnosis, and it appears to be much easier to do than ordinary remote viewing of a hidden object. This faculty might stem from the fact that I am looking at a living system whose name I know, and with whom I can resonate better than with a teddy bear in a box. My successes may also stem from the fact that diagnosis is inherently a more meaningful task than identifying objects and places. No one appears to know for sure, but all the medical intuitives I've spoken with agree with this last observation.

Psychic diagnosis of illness is similar to remote viewing in that the physical distance between the patient and the person doing the psychic diagnosis does not affect the accuracy of the diagnosis. Such distance may even be beneficial, because it prevents the intuitive practitioner from being bombarded by the analytical noise (referred to as "front-loading" in remote-viewing circles) that accompanies sensory input. In this chapter, I will describe the approaches to psychic diagnosis that seem to work for others, as well as those that work best for me.

AMERICA'S MOST FAMOUS PSYCHIC

Edgar Cayce gave distant medical diagnoses, suggested treatments, and offered character readings (called life readings) for more than thirty years. He was born in 1877 and died in 1943. He is best known for his more than 14,000 clairvoyant readings, of which 9,400 dealt with health issues. Cayce is perhaps equally famous for his prophecies and past-life readings.[1] To prepare himself for clairvoyant readings, Cayce would lie on a couch, close his eyes, and drop into a self-induced hypnotic trance. He would then listen to the name and address of the distant person and slowly, from within his trance, specify the body system or organ that was causing his client's illness. Then he would often suggest the remedy. Psychologist Gina Cerminara spent a year studying the Cayce documents at his foundation, The Association for Research and Enlightenment (ARE) in Virginia Beach, Virginia. In her book *Many Mansions,* she describes numerous astonishing cases in which Cayce described the exact condition or problem area — heart, liver, gall bladder, etcetera — of a distant sufferer and prescribed an herbal cure that was subsequently reported to be entirely effective.[2]

Cayce considered his entranced self to be a channel of higher consciousness. He believed that he obtained his information from the storehouse of universal information, known in ancient Eastern philosophy as the *akashic* record. Today we might say that, in our nonlocal universe, all information — past, present and future — is available to an open and expanded awareness. Cayce declared that his information came to him from a higher sense perception — an experience he shares with the contemporary energy healer Barbara Brennan (whose work I will discuss later). Cayce took a holistic, or systems, approach to health and disease. His readings dealt with the interrelationship of a person's environmental, mental, and physical factors. He was one of the first to speak of how the "intelligence" of the heart and the stomach (the enteric brain) affects the development of disease. For example, he suggested that chocolate, wine, and cheese could trigger migraines in susceptible people because of the vibrational properties of these foods. (Today we might say that this is because they are rich in MAO inhibitors, which interfere with the neurologically protective action of the body's own monoamine oxidase.)

Cayce received hundreds of requests for healing each week, and did up to six readings a day. Since his interest as a healer was in aiding the sick and reducing suffering, there was generally no follow-up on the efficacy of his diagnosis or his prescriptions. Although the ARE has these 9,400 readings available on a CD, I am sorry to say that they still await an in-depth, systematic evaluation.[3]

THE BODY'S ENERGY SYSTEMS

Dr. Judith Orloff is a practicing psychiatrist who also has a lifetime of experience with psychic functioning. As a child, she had a direct sense of when people were ill or when they were going to die. After finishing her medical training and residency at UCLA Medical School, she worked from time to time as a research partner and remote viewer with Stephen Schwartz at the Mobius Society in Los Angeles. Judith has been able to combine her natural gifts of sensing psychic vibrational energies with her experience as a remote viewer to augment her medical training with a significant amount of intuitive or psychic psychiatry. She describes her adventures, from her visionary girlhood to her present life as a Beverly Hills psychiatrist, in her captivating book *Second Sight*.[4] She also tells us about her highly successful remote viewing of distant targets.

I am grateful to Judith for relating her experiences in the world of vibrational energy perception, which is an ability I do not yet share. As she sits at her desk in her consulting room, she is able to integrate what the patient says to her with her own direct perception or experience of their body energy. In her new book, *Intuitive Healing,* Judith invites her students to picture their bodies in terms of the traditional energy centers known as chakras.[5] These emotional centers have been described for millennia in the Hindu tradition as seven individual energy vortices, spaced in levels from the bottom of the spine to the top of the head. Many of the well-known medical intuitives — but by no means all — experience the body in these terms. Edgar Cayce, for example, did not.

My first contact with this chakra system was in the 1960s, when I was investigating *kundalini* meditation. This is a meditative practice of breathing, visualization, and profound release of energy. I carefully read John Woodroffe's encyclopedic book, *The Serpent Power,* which described the chakras as the energetic "centers of serpent power."[6] This pioneering translation from nineteenth-century Sanskrit texts provided the Western world with copious and detailed information on the nature of the chakra system, as well as the meditative practices that have historically been associated with it. After six months of conscientious meditation, I achieved my long-sought energetic experience. It was the equivalent of having a white-hot poker run up the length of my spine and into my brain. As a result of this terrifying encounter with "the serpent," I am convinced that the image of chakra energy in not entirely metaphorical. But, although kundalini yoga practice offers a well-known opportunity to experience internal energy (or to burn out one's brains!), it does not necessarily lead to enlightenment. This would be another thing *not* to try at home without a teacher.

Dr. Orloff organizes these energetic and emotional centers as follows:

Chakra	Location	Function	Color
First	Genitals, anus	Sexuality, survival	Red
Second	2 inches below the navel	Sexuality, nurturing, balance	Orange
Third	Solar plexus	Emotional power, drive, need for control	Yellow
Fourth	Heart (2 inches above the diaphragm)	Compassion, love	Green
Fifth	Throat	Communication, speaking one's truth	Cobalt blue
Sixth (third eye)	Forehead, between the eyebrows	Intuition, intellect	Purple
Seventh (crown)	Top of the head	Spirituality	White

Dr. Orloff also teaches that, before one seeks either personal power or medical intuitive abilities, it is advisable to first spend time exploring one's own emotional and energetic fields. She offers a mind-quieting, introspective practice to help people learn to directly sense these energies. Her method is similar in many ways to the practice of *vipassana* meditation. This is an inward-looking insight meditation in which one does not shut out bodily sensations, but rather moves awareness into them, paying deep and abiding attention to each in turn. I had an opportunity to participate in a ten-day silent vipassana retreat with the compassionate, patient teacher Jack Kornfield, at his Spirit Rock Meditation Center in northern California. I discovered that just being quiet for ten days can be a life-changing experience in itself, not to mention the blessing of having a gifted teacher available.

In her book *Intuitive Healing,* Judith describes in detail how one might approach this insight meditation practice. Here is a sample:

- Find a comfortable position. Close your eyes. Take a few deep breaths. Relax. Gently focus your attention on your body.
- How does your body feel?
- Notice any physical discomfort or areas that are relaxed. Try to perceive your subtle energy.
- Do you have any waves of tingling or buzzing anywhere?
- Do you feel any rushes of heat, cold, or goose bumps, unrelated to the outside temperature?
- Can you pinpoint the specific organ involved?
- You may sense energy as a hum, a color, or a quivering. Some parts of your body may feel alive or especially sensitive — others dull, aching, or numb. Let your imagination go wild. You may feel sensation in places you never even knew existed. This is good.

From my long friendship with Judith, I would describe her as a loving, peaceful person longing to be quietly in touch with the Divine. There is an empathic element in the physical body of the intuitive, as well as a visual diagnostic aspect. In addition to her natural empathy and psychiatric training, Judith has extensive experience as a remote viewer. She is in touch with the phenomenology of discerning the psychic signal from the mental noise. Therefore, I trust her teaching. I believe that if you follow her practice, you cannot help but come into contact with the energetic elements of your own being. This is a very peaceful undertaking. There is no risk, and you can't be wrong; you are merely coming into contact with your own inner experience and activity. On the other hand, Dr. Mona Lisa Schultz, another psychiatrist and medical intuitive (discussed in the following section) is a risk-taker who invites you to come along with her into the unknown and see what you can discover outside your self.

WHAT IS A MEDICAL INTUITIVE?

In Judith's teaching, we understand that medical intuitives are sensitive to the subtle changes in their own and other people's bodies. This allows them to become aware of imbalances at an energetic level and to suggest changes in behavior, nutrition, or thought patterns before the imbalance manifests as an actual illness. Dr. Mona Lisa Schultz has succeeded in becoming sensitive to all the clues — psychic and nonpsychic — that provide information about the health of oneself or another person. This view of intuition comprises both psychically derived information and information perceived at a nonpsychic, subconscious level. This approach appears to be extremely valuable for a doctor, but it is not what I am primarily interested in here. I am investigating diagnosis at a distance, not across the desk (as Judith does), not across the waiting room (as later described by Dr. Karagulla) or in the emergency room (as Dr. Schultz so valuably does). However, to the best of my ability, I have not been able to find any instance of true double-blind intuitive medical diagnosis (apart from Edgar Cayce) in which the intuitive person is not looking at or talking to the patient, or to the patient's doctor. But I have successfully done this myself, and I will tell you how you can do it as well.

What It Takes to Be a Medical Intuitive

Mona Lisa Schultz is an M.D., Ph.D., psychiatrist, researcher, and fearless medical intuitive. As of 2001, you could call her on the telephone in Boston and tell her your name and age, and she would visualize your body, mind, and spirit and tell you what was troubling each of these systems.

Some doctors have the ability to diagnose illness in an instant (to make a snap diagnosis); as soon as you walk into their office, they intuitively know what's wrong with you. When Mona Lisa entered medical school at Boston University, she could instantly sense the medical problems afflicting the patients she was seeing. Mona Lisa did not seek out her gift. In fact, all through medical school she kept asking herself, "Why me?"

Based on her decade of work as a psychiatrist and medical intuitive, Mona Lisa has written a comprehensive manual to guide you on the path of distant medical diagnosis. Her book *Awakening Intuition* provides step-by-step instructions on how to sense and evaluate impressions of each of a patient's seven emotional centers.[7] She also offers a useful list of the properties of intuitive information. You will recognize that her list has all the elements we have come to associate with successful remote viewing. I think she is on the right track. Here is her list of general characteristics of intuitive information:

- Gestalt nature of knowing
- Certainty in the truth of intuitive insight
- Associated with empathy
- Suddenness and immediacy of knowledge
- Difficulty putting images into words
- Emotion/affect associated with the intuitive insight
- Nonanalytic, nonrational, nonlogical

The overall teaching of this list is that we must surrender to the experience; you can't push harder and harder to get a reading. In fact, it is clear from the writings of all the intuitives that medical diagnosis is a nonanalytical process, associated with feelings and visual images that are often metaphorical. Mona Lisa and Judith both have a great practical advantage over many other medical intuitives in that they are well trained in anatomy and physiology.

This means that when they see a gallbladder or a spleen on their mental screen, they know what they are looking at and can often name it.

Although I have taught remote viewing for many years, I have not taught intuitive diagnosis. During the past year, however, I have been learning to do intuitive diagnosis with surprising success, with the help of Katharyn Fenske, my patient teacher, who is a masseuse and a medical intuitive herself. I believe that you can learn to be an intuitive by following the approach I described in Chapter 3 and applying it to the system of emotional centers that Dr. Schultz describes in *Awakening Intuition*.

DEVELOPING YOUR INTUITIVE DIAGNOSTIC ABILITIES

Whatever approach you take to intuitive diagnosis, your progress will be greatly enhanced if you understand the underlying remote-viewing phenomenology that I've been discussing in this book. The next essential ingredient is a friend who will work with you; you can learn to be intuitives together.

Ask your friend to prepare file cards with the names of several patients and their symptoms (or other descriptors) for two or more friends. If your intuition partner can't think of two sick friends, it's okay to just choose two interesting or unusual people; we all know plenty of those.

Have your partner put the cards in separate identical envelopes so that neither of you knows which card is in which envelope. Then select one of the envelopes. This will be your "patient."

The reason for all this secrecy is that you don't want to train yourself to read the subtle clues from your partner in response to your intuitive descriptions. If your partner isn't "blind" to the target, he or she can't help but give you unconscious head nods or changes in breathing to indicate your successful intuitions. It is essential that you learn to discern intuitive data by yourself, because in a real situation you will not, of course, have a helper.

Part One: The Feeling Stage

With the target envelope in front of you, you want to achieve a single-pointed focus of attention and seriousness of purpose by saying to yourself or thinking, "I have a person who needs a description." You can then use the short insight meditation described by Dr. Orloff in the previous section, or use some other brief meditation technique to relax yourself.

Now you are ready to describe any bodily sensations, feelings, or experiences that pertain to the person described in the envelope. I prefer to speak aloud all my feelings and responses, rather that writing them down. I keep my eyes closed while my partner makes notes for me.

Part Two: The Visual Stage

In this phase, "visually" scan the body of the person in your mind's eye. I always scan from top to bottom, but I find in the literature that everybody else scans from the bottom up, in the order in which chakras are usually described. When you are new to this practice, your friend can slowly lead you through these centers, in whichever direction feels comfortable.

Dr. Schultz lists the seven centers as follows:

1. Physical body support, bones, joints, spine, blood, immunity
2. Uterus, ovaries, cervix, vagina, prostate, testes, bladder, large intestine, rectal area, lower back
3. Abdomen, middle digestive tract, liver, gallbladder, kidneys, spleen, middle spine

4. Heart, blood vessels, lungs, breasts
5. Neck, teeth, gums, thyroid
6. Brain, eyes, ears, nose
7. Genetic disorders, life-threatening illnesses, multiple organ involvement

You do not have to make a detailed mental investigation of each of these organs and systems, but you should pay some attention to each of the general areas so that you don't become fixated on one clearly discernible problem, while neglecting another that might also be serious. (This was a big temptation for me as a beginner; I was so happy to have actually seen something that I felt I was finished, when in reality I had only begun.)

Part Three: Gathering Additional Information

Since your partner doesn't know who your patient is, she can ask you questions to elicit more information from your subconscious, which is grappling with fragmentary pictures and feelings. She can ask you to say more about what you are experiencing or ask what you see that makes you say such-and-such. She might suggest taking a break and then going back to see what else you can see. "Are you sure you looked at all parts of the body?" is a good question.

RIGHT-BRAIN AND LEFT-BRAIN APPROACHES

What I've just described is a somewhat "left-brained," analytical approach, which is the way I tackle most problems, including remote viewing. When I started to get interested in medical diagnosis, the first thing I did was to purchase a set of twelve videotapes on anatomy and physiology from The Teaching Company.[8] The tapes covered the vascular, muscular, nervous, and endocrine systems. I felt that, in order to discern and describe what I was psychically looking at, I should be able to recognize and name it. All together,

I spent about forty hours with the videotapes, and I consider it one of the most worthwhile learning experiences of my life. Thus, if I were scanning a distant person I would now be able to say, "This person looks kind of pink all over. She feels warm to me. There is a bright redness on her right side, near her large intestine. I would guess that she has appendicitis." I would probably not feel her pain.

Other trainers, such as Prudence Calabrese at Trans Dimensional Systems or Wayne Carr at the Western Institute of Remote Viewing, take a more holistic approach. The right-brained (or nonanalytical) approach to the same reading I just described might stress feelings of fullness or even pain (which I did not report). It would definitely include impressions of the person's mental and emotional states (how the patient's life was going and what was weighing on that person's mind). One might sense a systemic problem and suggest that it be looked at by a doctor. But, in my experience, it is the ability to directly see and describe the affected system or systems that can motivate a patient to get medical help.

The difference in approaches probably comes from the fact that I am a man and a physicist, and Doctors Orloff and Schultz are both women psychiatrists with a much more compassionate, holistic approach. My training as a remote viewer "from Mars" makes me look for the broken piece so that it can be fixed. On the other hand, Judith and Mona Lisa, "from Venus," take a general systems view of the whole mind, body, and spirit. This is beyond my present capability. My approach will generally not be sensitive to emotional problems, or to whether the person is getting a divorce or fighting with the boss.

MY EXPERIENCE WITH MEDICAL DIAGNOSIS

In my own first trial, my teacher Katharyn Fenske, an experienced healer, gave me an envelope that contained a card describing a person she knew. (It was not one of my double-blind trials; I didn't realize the importance of these until after that first trial.) I closed my eyes and quieted my mind. I then began a mental scan of the target person's body, from top to bottom. My process doesn't involve looking at chakras, although it appears that almost everyone else's does. I got to the person's midsection and, much to my surprise, I saw a highly illuminated pancreas — just like the anatomical drawings on my videotapes. In my mental view, it was an alarming orange and yellow color, instead of the pleasant pink of the tapes. I said, "I see an isolated pancreas. It looks orange and yellow. It doesn't look good. Does this person have diabetes?" The answer was "yes." I also realized that I'd made a very fast rush to judgment; the whole body should be scanned before making any such analytic statement.

We took a break, after which Katharyn asked me if I could see anything else. This time I scanned the whole body for about five minutes. It all looked okay, but at the top of the nice blue spinal column, there were three greenish vertebrae. I reported this, and asked if the person had a problem with her spine. (I always have an immediate flash about the gender of the patient, which is almost always correct, though I was once fooled by a particularly masculine woman athlete.) The answer was again "yes." I later learned that this person was receiving massage treatments from Katharyn, for help in recovering from whiplash. It appears that I was not seeing into the body but, rather, responding intuitively to something in the body system, which then illuminated the appropriate icon for me from my anatomy lessons!

Three weeks later, in a similar trial with Katharyn, I was scanning the athletic woman whom I mistook for a man. I saw a small, hunched-over person with short dark hair, and no evidence of a problem except that the aorta kept coming into view. As I looked at it, the red blood cells appeared convex, rather than concave as they should be, and there didn't seem to be very many of them. I offered that the person was depressed and possibly anemic. No talk of relationships, childhood abuse, or faltering self-esteem — just the facts! Both of these observations turned out to be correct. In a final scan, I saw a small, isolated, bright-red patch on her left shoulder. My interviewer couldn't confirm anything like that. She called the patient (who lived in Florida), and learned that she did not currently have a problem with her left shoulder, but that she did have a metal plate in that location dating from when she had been a tennis player and had a shoulder separation.

I have been practicing intuitive medical diagnosis for about a year now, and I find it much easier than remote viewing. Other experienced intuitives all agree with that assessment.

ARE THERE ANY DATA?

Through my association with the New York Theosophical Society in the 1950s, I had an opportunity to meet and work with Dora Kunz, a renowned clairvoyant and healer. Dora became the president of the American Theosophical Society in 1975, and she taught healing to Dolores Krieger. Together, they originated the Therapeutic Touch healing method. Kunz's remarkable higher-sense perceptions, or visualizations of auras, are described in the book *Breakthrough to Creativity.*[9] My work with Kunz was rather superficial. I was only twenty-two years old, and had just been introduced to the ideas of biological energy fields, which feature prominently in the writings of Theosophy and the work of physicist Hans Richenbach. I wanted to see if Dora could directly sense magnetic fields from hidden magnets, as some of Richenbach's psychic subjects could do. I found that Dora could indeed locate hidden magnets, and she could even tell whether the north or south pole was facing her.[10]

Ten years later, Dora found a more appropriate scientist to

work with. She teamed up with Dr. Shafrica Karagulla, who made a careful study of Dora's psychic diagnostic abilities. Karagulla's 1967 book[11] is the first attempt to scientifically investigate a gifted medical intuitive. Dr. Karagulla describes her approach:

> Day after day, Diane [really Dora] and I followed our routine of selecting a patient at random, with no knowledge of his medical background. We sat quietly in the waiting room of the Endocrine Clinic while she made her observations and I wrote down my notes. One afternoon I pointed to a patient sitting in chair number five, and Diane began to describe an abnormal condition of the pituitary gland. She found the vortex of energy in the immediate vicinity slow in movement....

Although we have many breathtaking descriptions of illness hidden from obvious view, it is impossible to assess what is actually going on. If a psychic looks at a person sitting in a chair reading his newspaper, and announces correctly that he has a pituitary tumor, what are we to think? We can certainly conclude that she has exceptional discernment, but what part of that discernment involves perceiving the disturbed energy fields she describes, and what part involves psychic contact with the person? We cannot determine that — at least I cannot. Dora's descriptions are almost always presented in terms of a colorful web of frequencies — the vital and energetic field of the body — and they are almost always correct. Twenty years later, a whole school was formed to teach this system.

Prominent New York healer Barbara Brennan teaches her students to scan their clients' energy fields to find "imbalances, tears, stagnations, and depletions" in their flow of energy. At the healing school she founded, she teaches students to use a "high sense perception" to observe their clients' auras. Students learn to watch the client's constantly changing flow of energy, which is undetectable by normal vision. Brennan attempts to teach this clairvoyant perception to her students so that they may use it in their healing practices, both to diagnose clients' problems and to rebalance and recharge the clients' energy fields (or *auras*). In her book *Hands of Light,* Brennan beautifully illustrates the shapes and colors of the energy imbalances she sees.[12] Brennan was formerly employed as a physicist at NASA, where she studied the reflection of solar light from the earth. Her knowledge of spectroscopy allows her a rare specificity in talking about people's auras. When she described to me a person's energy field as measured in hundreds of nanometers (10^{-9} meters), she got this laser physicist's undivided attention!

Barbara Brennan, Jane Katra, and I had a very amiable meeting in New York City several years ago. At least it became amiable after we left the incredible noise and confusion of the venerable Stage Delicatessen, where I foolishly took everyone for lunch. Barbara wanted to learn something about remote viewing, and Jane and I were, of course, interested in her energy perceptions. Barbara hid an object of her choosing in the bathroom of our hotel room and asked me describe it. As I sat above the noisy city and quieted my thoughts, Barbara interrupted me by saying, "I can see that your thought beams are in contact with my object right now! Just describe what you are seeing." I went on to describe a small red object with spines sticking out of it; each spine had a little knob on it. That turned out to be a quite satisfactory description of the object: her hairbrush. In addition, I was very impressed — and remain impressed — that Barbara could confidently and correctly see a "beam of light" corresponding to where my attention was directed. If I ever need to have my energy vortices untangled and combed straight, I believe she is the one who could do it.

FIFTY CASES OVER THE PHONE

In the 1980s, physician Norman Shealy and his sensitive research partner, Caroline Myss, carried out a definitive series of distant diagnosis trials. In previous years, they had cooperated in numerous diagnostic experiments in which Caroline described the psychological problems of Shealy's patients. When they became interested in formally documenting her remarkable diagnostic abilities, they decided to carry out a fifty-trial series over the telephone. Caroline would not see the patients, but would be given the name and birth date of the patient sitting in Dr. Shealy's consulting room. This remarkable series is described in the book *Creation of Health*, coauthored by Shealy and Myss.[13] Shealy reports that Caroline had an overall accuracy of 93 percent in her assessments over the telephone!

In *Creation of Health*, Shealy and Myss published a table summarizing this landmark experiment. In one column, they listed Dr. Shealy's diagnosis of the patient after a medical examination. In the other column, they recorded what Caroline had to say from her publishing office, 1,500 miles away. What follows is a portion of that table:

Patient	Caroline's Intuitive Diagnosis	C. N. Shealy's Medical Diagnosis
1	Schizophrenic, disturbed sexuality	Schizophrenic, very disturbed sexuality
2	Migraine headache, myofacial pain	Migraine headache, myofacial pain
3	Depression, sexual problems	Depression, sexual problems
4	Venereal herpes	Venereal herpes
48	Back pain, anxiety	Post-surgical back pain, anxiety
49	Wasting of the brain	Alzheimer's
50	Electrical storms in the brain	Epilepsy

Shealy says, "I have not seen anyone more accurate than Caroline, not even a physician." I believe that this research on distant diagnosis, together with the work I describe in the next chapter on distant healing, will change the shape and direction of medicine in the decades to come. We will learn how to inflow information about the world that is distant from us in space and time. We will also learn how to outflow our prayers and healing intentions to bring increased health to those who are sick and in need of help. The evidence for this capability of distant healing is already appearing in prominent U.S. medical journals, describing clinical studies in hospitals. Now that we are solidly in the new millennium, we are experiencing in every area of human activity what Marianne Williamson calls "a climax in which science and religion are becoming coherent in the exclamation of a single, unified truth. It will finally be recognized and appreciated that the direct experience of spirituality is not at all in conflict with a rational and scientific pursuit of our lives."[14]

distant

healing

IS IT MY MIND OVER YOUR MATTER?

. . . the works that I do, shall you do also;
and greater works than these shall you do.

— John, 14:12

The previous chapters have dealt with our ability to inflow information about something hidden, distant, or in the future. In this chapter, I will describe the best available information showing that we can outflow our energy or healing intentions to alleviate suffering or pain.

Since the earliest of times, communities of people have recognized certain individuals in their midst who possessed a special gift for healing, from Native American shamans to Hindu gurus. The founders of the world's great religions, Buddha, Jesus, and Mohammed, were all reported to have been gifted healers. Jesus was the best known of all spiritual healers, and he inspired the first generations of Christians to practice healing in community.[1] Jesus said that any who were willing to surrender to a higher power could learn to become healers, whether or not they were Christians.[2]

When someone says to you, "I'll keep you in my prayers," what do they really have in mind? Why does it give us a warm feeling to know that someone is thinking kindly of us? Why should we care? I believe we know intuitively that the distant loving intentions of a friend are somehow helpful. In Chapter 4, I described the carefully conducted experiments of Helmut Schmidt, which showed that the thoughts of one person can affect the breathing rate of another person at an earlier time. These results are astonishing because they throw into question our understanding of the dimension of time, as well as our basic understanding of causality.

In order to explore similar questions regarding the nature of distant healing, we must answer two distinct and critical questions: What is the evidence that the one person's thoughts can actually affect or heal the physical body of another person who is not in close proximity? And, equally important, what are the expectations of the person being healed?

Further, if we are convinced that we have a fundamental tripartite nature, comprising equal measures of body, mind, and spirit, which of these elements do we hope the healer will affect? The answer we find most congenial will probably depend on whether we are working with an energy healer, a psychic healer, a spiritual healer, or someone entirely different.[3]

Just as contemporary physicists grapple with the role of consciousness in the physical world, health practitioners debate the extent to which the mind affects the health of the body. In this chapter, I will describe several ways in which one person's mind, directed with healing intentions, may affect another person's health — how mind-to-mind connections can facilitate "energy healing" as well as distant psychic and spiritual healing. I will discuss the human capacity to stabilize and direct our attention to outflow our prayers, our energy, and our healing intentions to bring increased health to the sick and those in need.

In his book *Meaning and Medicine*, visionary physician Larry Dossey asks:

> How do prayer, noncontact therapeutic touch, extended effects of meditation, effects of transpersonal or distant imagery, and diagnosis at a distance fit into modern medicine? Can they fit? I believe the answer is yes, if we are bold enough to extend our views of the mind.[4]

OLD-STYLE HYPNOSIS

Though it wasn't specifically related to distant healing, my first personal contact with intentional mental influence was in 1969, when the distinguished Czech researcher and hypnotist Milan Ryzl visited our Parapsychology Research Group in Portola Valley, California. This group of friends and researchers has been meeting continuously since 1965, when I founded it with psychologist Charles Tart, philosophy professor Jeffrey Smith, and consciousness researcher Arthur Hastings. Over the years, our little group has had visits from many ESP luminaries, including J. B. Rhine, J. G. Pratt, and Hugh Lynn Cayce.

A Visit From Milan Ryzl

On the occasion of Milan Ryzl's visit, fifty people were gathered in Jeffrey Smith's spacious, rock-walled living room, where we were treated to a demonstration of what I think of as the old-fashioned "master-slave" approach to mental influence. Until recent years, this authoritarian approach was popular among hypnotists, especially in Eastern Europe.

Dr. Ryzl, a chemical engineer, achieved fame in parapsychology circles for his amazingly successful clairvoyance experiments, in which he psychically communicated fifteen numbers (decimal digits) to a gifted psychic.[5] His research goal was to achieve perfect accuracy in sending a message, and his results were among the most striking in the annals of psi research. To accomplish his objective, Ryzl had an assistant randomly select five groups of numbers, of three digits each. The fifteen decimal digits were then encoded into binary form (combinations of ones and zeros) and translated into a sequence of fifty green or white cards (with green representing "one" and white representing "zero"), which were each then placed in an opaque, sealed envelope. In this experiment, Ryzl worked with an exceptional hypnotic subject named Pavel Stepanek. Through use of a redundant coding technique, requiring almost 20,000 psychic calls for green or white cards (one or zero), Ryzl transmitted all fifteen digits to Stepanek without error (odds of 10^{-15}).

At our 1969 California gathering, Ryzl graciously agreed to demonstrate his highly successful approach, and he asked for a volunteer to be a hypnotic subject. We were all eager to see his technique in action. However, he shocked all of us — especially the young woman volunteer — when, after the lights were dimmed, he declaimed to her, "My will overcomes your will. You will do exactly as I say!" Though his approach was surprising, it was also very effective. The picture-drawing experiment he demonstrated that night (which can be seen as a form of remote viewing) was completely successful. We were able to see how he had achieved his great success in the experiment with Stepanek a decade before anyone had even heard of remote viewing. Today, hypnosis has become a much more widely known, expansive, and cooperative undertaking.

Franz Mesmer's Pioneering Role

In 1779, the charismatic German physician Franz Mesmer was the first person to systematically and scientifically investigate hypnosis and the healing of a person purely through the intentions of another. Although this sort of healing had been going on since the dawn of humanity, it appears that Mesmer was the first doctor to recognize and describe the importance of strong rapport and a mind-to-mind connection with his patients. Mesmer achieved this connection through the use of rhythmic, "magnetic" passes over their body until they became entranced — often for more than an hour. He also was the first to conjecture that psychological trauma might be a cause of physical illness.

Vasiliev's Hypnosis Research

In the 1920s and 1930s, Leonid Leonidovich Vasiliev was a pioneering Soviet researcher in psychology and physiology, following in the tradition of Franz Mesmer. His specialty was the treatment of hysterical symptoms using hypnosis. He was, however, alternately in and out of favor with the ruling Stalinist regime. When he was supported by Stalin, he directed the Leningrad Institute for Brain Research, founded by his teacher V. M. Bekhterev to investigate hypnosis for the treatment of hysterical illnesses. For a time in the early 1930s, his research was considered too spiritual and he was out of work. But by 1933, Vasiliev was back at his old institute with a proper materialist program to investigate the effects of electromagnetic shielding on the induction of hypnosis.

Apart from the treatment of illness and the relief of pain through hypnosis, Vasiliev's principal interest was the induction of sleep through hypnosis. He used the signature approach of the stage hypnotist: "You are feeling sleepy. Your eyelids are getting very heavy." Vasiliev was surprised to find that his best hypnotic subjects sometimes dropped off into a hypnotic sleep when he only thought these words.[6] His most famous subsequent experiments involved the induction of sleep and wakefulness at greater and greater distances, up to many miles from his hypnotic subject. After many initial experiments in distant sleep, with blindfolded subjects in the laboratory and homebound patients watched by their landladies, he began formal experiments with subjects under tight laboratory controls such as we might use today.

To examine the effects of strict electromagnetic shielding, Vasiliev constructed a steel test chamber, about six feet on a side, lined with lead and sealed with a mercury-filled trough (something we would not do today). To determine the wakefulness of a subject inside the chamber, Vasiliev asked her to squeeze a rubber bulb each time she took a breath. The air blown out of the bulb was conveyed by a copper tube through the chamber wall to a pneumatic recording device that marked a chart each time the woman squeezed the bulb. Vasiliev describes two of his hysterical medical patients, Ivanova and Fedorova, as exceptional hypnotic subjects. While under hypnosis, they could accurately draw what he was drawing and even taste substances he was tasting.

Vasiliev carried out these experiments by climbing into a second shielded enclosure in a distant room. Then, on a preset schedule, he would visualize and will his patient to either fall asleep or awaken from sleeping. He observed that, within a few seconds to a minute after his mental sleep-induction began, the squeezing of the bulb would cease. Then, at the appropriate time, he would attempt to awaken the sleeping subject and the marks on the moving chart would begin again, indicating that she had indeed awakened and resumed squeezing the bulb. Vasiliev repeated these experiments with many variations, and demonstrated them to the Soviet Academy of Sciences. His great excitement over these results stemmed from the fact that the onset of sleep or awakening did not differ at all, with or without shielding. This showed conclusively that the medium of telepathic transmission could not be any known form of electromagnetic waves.

For me, the most exciting of Vasiliev's experiments are his long-distance hypnosis trials, in which he rules out any possibility of sensory leakage to his subjects. In these experiments, Vasiliev's research partner, Professor Tomashevsky, was sent to Sevastopol (one thousand miles from Leningrad) to be the telepathic sender. While there, Tomashevsky would exert his will as an experienced hypnotist to create a controlling influence on the subject back in the laboratory during prearranged two-hour experimental periods. The actual times of sleep and awakening were unknown to Leningrad observers. Their watches were synchronized with Radio Moscow, and the observed times of sleep and awakening for these well-trained hypnotic subjects were again within one minute of the onset of the sender's mental influence. An accidental control trial was inserted when Tomashevsky, the sender, became ill one day. There was no hypnotic intention in Sevastopol that day, and no appearance of hypnotic induction was observed during the entire two-hour experimental period in Leningrad.

Ever since my first reading of Vasiliev's remarkable book, *Experiments in Mental Suggestion,* in the 1960s, I have often reflected on the haunting image of his patients, usually sick women, some partially paralyzed, huddled in his dark steel cubicle obediently squeezing their little rubber bulbs, waking and falling asleep like little birds as the walls of the chamber exuded a toxic miasma of mercury vapor from their seams. Some day there will be such a movie. But there is no doubt that Vasiliev's three decades of careful research provide convincing evidence that the thoughts of one person can, indeed, affect the behavior of another person at a distance. I believe that the rather disturbing domination of the will described here occurs only between an experienced hypnotist and a completely cooperative and experienced subject.

This is another example of something you should probably not try at home.

These voodoo-like experiments, coming to us from early in the last century, may appear shocking by modern research standards. To this mild-mannered physicist, however, the observation that the efficacy of the mind-to-mind connection is independent of both distance and electromagnetic shielding sounds remarkably contemporary — simply another nonlocal connection. Presenting the most modern view on this subject, the eminent physicist Henry Stapp of the University of California at Berkeley writes:

> [T]he new physics presents prima facie evidence that our human thoughts are linked to nature by nonlocal connections: What a person chooses to do in one region seems immediately to affect what is true elsewhere in the universe. This nonlocal aspect can be understood by conceiving the universe to be, not a collection of tiny bits of matter, but rather a growing compendium of "bits of information".... And I believe that most quantum physicists will also agree that our conscious thoughts ought eventually to be understood within science and that, when properly understood, our thoughts will be seen to do something: *They will be efficacious* (emphasis in original).7

REPEATABLE MIND-TO-BODY CONNECTIONS

Since Vasiliev's pioneering research, many investigators have sought a reliable and sensitive way to demonstrate that the thoughts of one person can manifest directly in the physiology of a distant person. This is a much more objective indication of thought transference than a telepathic response, which has to be mediated through the receiver's conscious awareness and then verbally reported or drawn.

In 1965, two years after the publication of Vasiliev's book in

English, chemist Douglas Dean of the Newark College of Engineering showed conclusively that the autonomic nervous systems of subjects in his laboratory directly responded to the thoughts of a distant person.[8] Douglas was a charming, openhearted Englishman who worked tirelessly to achieve recognition for parapsychology research. He and Margaret Mead were the people most responsible for getting the prestigious American Association for the Advancement of Science (AAAS) to accept the Parapsychology Association, of which he was president, with full standing in 1969.

In Dean's experiments, participant receivers lay quietly on a cot in a darkened room, while an optical plethysmograph[9] with a small light bulb and a photocell recorded changes in their fingers' blood volume, which is a measure of autonomic nervous system activity. In these highly repeatable experiments, the sender was seated at a table in another room. At a signal from a light flash, the sender would look at randomly ordered cards with names on them at the rate of one card per minute. The autonomic activity of the distant receiver (who was connected to the plethysmograph) was observed to increase markedly when the sender focused on cards with names that had personal or emotional significance for the receiver (parent, spouse, sweetheart, dog), as compared with random names from the telephone book. While the receiver's heartbeats were registered one by one during the course of a twenty-minute session, he or she was unaware of when significant names were being observed by the sender. With some subjects, the difference between the two conditions was so strong that the changes in pulse shape on the recording chart could be directly observed without any sophisticated analysis.

DISTANT MENTAL INFLUENCE

Dr. William Braud at the Institute of Transpersonal Psychology (ITP) in Palo Alto, California, has worked for more than three decades to achieve an understanding of what we loosely call "distant mental influence." Braud, often collaborating with Dr. Marilyn Schlitz (now research director at the Institute of Noetic Science in Petaluma, California), carried out dozens of experiments investigating a person's ability to directly influence the subtle psychological behavior of people in distant rooms using mental means alone. These experiments included efforts to remotely influence a person's blood pressure and state of relaxation, as measured by the electrical resistance changes of the skin (galvanic skin response, or GSR). Other studies involved trying to increase the activity rate of gerbils running on a wheel, and influencing the spontaneous swimming direction of small electric knife fish (a type of carp). All of these experiments examining mental influence at a distance were successful, and — most importantly — repeatable.[10]

Braud's theory is that labile systems — living things that exhibit some level of activity — are easier to move or affect than systems at rest, which exhibit a high degree of inertia. This is a kind of psychological statement of Newton's third law, which says that objects in motion tend to stay in motion, and objects at rest tend to remain at rest. Dr. J. B. Rhine, in his efforts to demonstrate mental influence in the 1940s, also recognized that it is easier to affect the trajectory of falling dice than it is to levitate dice that are resting on the table.

Braud was very selective in the systems he studied. If the creatures were not labile enough, or were sluggish, it might be too difficult to get them started. On the other hand, if an animal's normal behavior was very near the activity ceiling, the animal might be showing nearly all the action one could expect from it. A gerbil, for instance, would be a better target than a snail or slug, or a hummingbird or bee; it would be hard to get the snail's attention, and similarly difficult to increase the activity level of the hummingbird.

Although most of Braud's highly successful work involved increasing and decreasing the degree of relaxation of people at a distant location, one of his most important experiments involved trying to psychically come to the aid of threatened red blood cells. In all of his other experiments with living systems, the creature (even the goldfish) had a level of consciousness that could, in principle, be affected by a distant person.[11]

In the following experiments, subjects in the laboratory were asked to influence the behavior of red blood cells, which to the best of our knowledge have no independent consciousness. In these studies, the cells were put into test tubes of distilled water, which is a toxic environment for them. If the salt content of the solution deviates too much from that of blood plasma, the cell wall weakens and the contents of the blood cell goes into the solution. This unfortunate situation is dispassionately called "hemolysis." The degree of hemolysis is easily measured; the transmission of light through a solution containing intact blood cells is much lower than the transmission through a solution of dissolved cells. During the experiment, a spectrophotometer was used to measure the light transmission as a function of time.

In each series with thirty-two different subjects, twenty tubes of blood were compared for each person. The subjects, situated in a distant room, had the task of attempting to save the little corpuscles from aqueous destruction in ten of the target tubes. The blood cells in the ten control tubes had to fend for themselves. Braud found that the people working as remote healers were able to significantly retard the hemolysis of the blood in the tubes they were trying to protect.[12]

These experiments are important because the mind of the subject/healer was able to directly interact with a living system, and one could not reasonably say that it was due to the placebo effect or a charming bedside manner. Another striking finding in these experiments was the fact that the participants who produced the most statistically significant results were even more successful in protecting their own blood cells than they were at preserving the life of cells that came from another person. This result is open to interpretation. It may be that, if psychic functioning is viewed as a kind of resonance, one is more in resonance with a part of oneself than with a part of another person. In his book *Distant Mental Influence*, Braud summarizes this idea:

> Concisely stated, the evidence compiled indicates that, under certain conditions, it is possible to know and to influence the thoughts, images, feelings, behaviors, and physiological and physical activities of other persons and living organisms — even when the influencer and the influenced are separated by great distances in space and time, beyond the reach of the conventional senses.[13]

Mental Influence via Television

Additional studies by Braud and Schlitz showed that if a person simply attended fully to a distant person whose physiological activity was being monitored, he or she could influence that person's autonomic galvanic skin responses. In four separate experiments involving seventy-six sessions, the active participant sat in an office cubicle and stared intently, off and on according to a set of randomized instructions, at a closed-circuit TV-monitor image of the distant person. This intermittent staring was enough to significantly influence the remote person's electrodermal (GSR) responses. The person who was stared at simply sat quietly, resting or meditating with closed eyes. No intentional focusing or mental imaging techniques were used by the influencer, other than staring at the "staree's" image on the video screen during randomly interspersed staring periods.

In these studies, Braud and Schlitz also discovered that the most anxious and introverted people being stared at had the greatest magnitude of unconscious electrodermal responses. In other words, the more shy and introverted people reacted with significantly more stress than did the sociable and extroverted people.

This experiment gives scientific validation to the common human experience of feeling stared at and turning around to find that someone is, indeed, staring at you.[14]

Marilyn Schlitz and Stephen LaBerge, at the U.S.-government-funded laboratory of Science Applications International Corporation (SAIC) in Menlo Park, California, successfully replicated Braud and colleagues' experiments, making some interesting changes in the protocol. In 1993, they again measured the extent to which people unconsciously sense the telepathic influence of a distant person who is looking at their video image. Again, the two participants were only briefly acquainted. In these studies, however, the observer was instructed to try to excite or startle the person whose video image they were staring at. This work differed from the previous work by Braud and Schlitz; in the earlier studies, the influencers were instructed simply to stare at the video image without trying to influence the "staree" directly; in the latter experiment the influencers were specifically trying to increase the stress response of the recipient.[15]

I believe that people have known about this phenomenon since the time of the ancient Greeks. Specifically, if a man stares at a woman's back in a theater, she will turn around and look at him. But let's not dwell on sorcery, aggressive uses of psychic abilities, or the potential need for psychic self-defense. Once you are reasonably physically fit and mentally freed from the trap of fear, judgment, and conditioned awareness, none of these potential hazards will be actual threats — just one more reason to get on with the discovery of who you really are.

Is It Really Mental Influence?

When Braud began this line of research, he believed that it could be viewed as a kind of biofeedback study. That is, he believed that the starers could learn to increase their effect on the starees by observing the GSR tracing on the polygraph chart showing the increases and decreases in electrical activity of the distant starees. He called this *allo-biofeedback* because it is feedback between two people. As we know, these experiments were highly successful. But it turned out that the feedback to the starer was neither necessary nor even helpful. Surprisingly, the starers were not able to improve their success by watching the GSR fluctuations of the distant person and modifying their strategies to see what worked. That is, there was no learning of how to be a better influencer, as we see in ordinary biofeedback training.

This is a perplexing result, and it weakens the supposed cause-and-effect relationship between the intention of the starer and the observed outcome. If I cannot improve my performance by observing the results of my effort, it casts doubt on the biological psychokinesis (Bio-PK) model, which holds that my mind directly affects your matter. It has implications for healers as well — if what they are doing is similar to distant mental influence. We don't even know whether it is the influencer (or healer) who is causing the changes. Many spiritual healers insist they are not the ones doing the healing. (The energy healers, on the other hand, seem to feel that it is they, indeed, who have the action.) If what is happening is not Bio-PK, then perhaps it is also not distant mental influence at all! We might describe the relationship as more of a "mutual co-arising or interaction over no distance," rather than a "doing."

Braud now considers this highly reliable class of experiments to be "direct mental interactions with living systems" (DMILS). This research has clearly demonstrated that there is a significant relationship between one person's intention and something happening with, or to, a distant living system. Also, since there is no change in success rate with increasing or decreasing distance in these experiments, they appear to fall into the nonlocal category, as does remote viewing — a direct interaction rather than a distant influence.

After three decades of research, Braud proposes that we profoundly reassess our view of the phenomena in which he was the pioneering researcher. He writes:

> This substitution [of interaction for influence] is made to remove the presumption or conclusion that the process is essentially an active psychokinetic, influential one, with an influencer again playing a major role. Interactions suggest that other psi processes — such as telepathy, clairvoyance, and precognition — may be involved as much as, or even to a greater extent than, psychokinesis; that the influencee might play a much more important — and cooperative — role than is immediately obvious; and that in all these experiments we are left [primarily] with correlations between influencer intentions, and influencee activities.[16]

This view is consistent with the assertions of the spiritual healer who considers herself to be an instrument of healing, rather than a person who is zapping distant patients to make them well.

Mental Influence on Nonliving Systems

Uri Geller, the Israeli magician and psychic who is famous for his purported ability to bend spoons without touching them, visited our laboratory at SRI in the winter of 1972. Geller was a delightful guest, and was unusually kind and patient with my little children who clamored for his attention. Many people think that Geller is a total fraud, and that he fooled us with his tricks.

But that is not true. We had more SRI technical and management oversight of our experiments with Uri than in any other phase of our research. Hal Puthoff and I found that, in carefully controlled experiments, Uri could psychically perceive and copy pictures that an artist and I randomly selected and drew while we were in an opaque, electrically shielded room. Geller's excellent drawings appear in our technical paper in *Nature,* and in our book, *Mind Reach.*[17] If we consider Geller's general ESP picture-drawing experiments to be a type of remote viewing, we could say that Geller was an excellent remote viewer, but by no means the best we saw at SRI.

Despite these successful perception experiments, we have widely reported that Uri did not psychically bend any metal at SRI. For two decades, I denigrated the whole spoon-bending craze as a kind of silliness. In the past year, however, I have seen some metal-bending that has changed my mind. My friend Jack Hauk is an aeronautical engineer at McDonnell Douglas Aircraft Company. He conducts spoon-bending parties, which he calls PK (psychokinesis) parties. At these parties, he guides and cheers party-goers to summon their supposed metal-bending psychic abilities and cause spoons to bend. I have seen lots of bent spoons, but I never saw anything that appeared significant or paranormal at these parties — at least not until 1999.

At a PK party in a Palo Alto hotel ballroom, Jack and I were attempting to videotape paranormal metal-bending — an effort that almost always ends in failure. As we were cleaning up after another disappointing event, we heard a shriek from the corner of the ballroom; it was Jane Katra. She had been sitting quietly, meditating with a silver-plated teaspoon in her fist, when suddenly the spoon came alive in her hand and shocked her out of her reverie. She described it as suddenly feeling that there was a cricket wiggling against the palm of her hand; that's what made her scream.

As several of us rushed over to see what had happened, we saw her looking at a very strange-looking spoon. While in her hand, the bowl of the spoon had rolled up 180 degrees toward the handle. We photographed the spoon and put it into a plastic bag. By the time we reached home, the spoon had rolled up to 270 degrees, and now looked like a little nautilus shell. That is, the actual bowl of the spoon, not the handle, rolled up. I can think of no way, by manual force or laboratory technology, that anyone could have accomplished this — certainly not Jane, who has small-boned little hands that have been bruised by just cutting roses.

The following month I attended a second PK party. This time, I was successful in bending a $3/8$-inch-diameter, foot-long aluminum rod by about thirty degrees. As I sat with my eyes closed, meditating, the bar became springy in my hands — then it bent! I brought an identical bar home for my two athletic sons to try to bend. Neither of these tall, strong oarsmen could bend it at all.

I am not relating these stories to indicate any psychic prowess on Jane's or my part. Rather, I think it is important to finally report that there is such a thing as paranormal metal-bending, and that it doesn't require Uri Geller to do it. The corollary to this is that if Jane and I can bend metal at a PK party, then it is quite likely that Geller, who invented this craze, can do it also. The fact that a stage magician can do mental magic or phony spoon-bending on the *Tonight Show* does not prove that these things do not actually occur.

THREE ERAS OF HEALING

Larry Dossey is one of the foremost pathfinders in the exploration of the spiritual dimensions of healing. Recently, his commitment to the study of mind-body healing has led him to become the executive editor of the new journal *Alternative Therapies in Health and Medicine.* In his inspiring books, *Recovering the Soul, Meaning and Medicine,* and *Healing Words,* Dossey describes three distinct types of healing methodology that have been used throughout the course of medical science.[18] Since they generally fall into historical sequence, he refers to these healing categories as "eras." Dossey's ideas provide a helpful framework for understanding the relationship between remote viewing and healing, so I will describe the three types of methodologies here.

In healing Era I, all forms of therapy are physical and the body is regarded as a mechanism that functions according to deterministic principles. Classical laws of matter and energy, as described by Newtonian physics, guide these approaches to healing, which focus solely on the effects of material forces on the physical body. The Era I approach to healing encompasses most of "modern" medical technology, and includes techniques such as drugs, surgery, and radiation. It also includes CPR, acupuncture, nutrition, and herbal medicine — but mind is not regarded as a healing factor in this era.

Dossey extols the accomplishments of Era I medicine in the history of healing, just as modern physicists acknowledge the contributions of Newtonian physics to our understanding of the laws of the physical universe. "These achievements are so significant that most persons believe the future of medicine still lies solidly in Era-I approaches," says Dossey, despite the fact that "all the major diseases of our day — heart disease, hypertension, cancer, and more — have now been shown to be influenced, at least to some degree, by the mind." A similar situation exists in the field of physics, in which the classical models persist although their proponents are unable to account for the data of relativity, quantum physics, or remote viewing.

Era II, according to Dossey, describes the mind-to-body medical approaches that involve the psychosomatic effect of one's consciousness on one's own body — the idea that what you think affects your health. Era-II medicine acknowledges a causal effect of the mind, but the mind is still seen as a function of brain chemistry and anatomy. Era II recognizes the connection between an individual's brain, mind, and organs. Its therapies involve psychosomatic medicine, and they include counseling, hypnosis, biofeedback, and self-healing imagery and relaxation techniques, as well as psychoneuroimmunology. Eras I and II are similar in that the mind is still considered to be localized in one's body, as well as in present time.

In the 1990s, we entered Era III of medical therapies. Despite the important advances of Era II medicine, researchers have recognized that it is incomplete. In Era III medicine, mind is seen as unconfined by either space (brains or bodies) or time (present experience). We recognize that our nonlocal mind may affect healing both within and between people. Noncontact healing modalities between people in each other's presence, as well as between people distant from each other, become possible with nonlocal mind. It is this latter element — distance — that distinguishes Era-III medicine. Dossey summarizes the situation as follows:

> After scrutinizing this body of data for almost two decades, I have come to regard it as one of the best-kept secrets in medical science. I'm convinced that the distant, nonlocal effects are real and that healing happens.[19]

Healing modalities from all three of these categories can be highly efficacious in certain situations and under the right conditions. The greater range of therapies that has become available with each new era of medicine has not extinguished the value of the healing methodologies of another era. Instead, each era's healing therapies complement the approaches used in the others. Many people don't understand this, and think that one mode must be sacrificed in order to use the other.

Modes of Healing

What kinds of healing do we see in Era-III medicine? Laying on of hands is probably the oldest form of healing in either traditional or nontraditional medicine. We find it in the Bible, and we find it in the present-day practice of Reiki. I had the privilege of taking a class in hands-on energy healing with Bernard Gunther, a master in this art, at the Esalen Institute many years ago. Bernard has learned how to stay focused on the compassionate give and take of energy with a patient, and he teaches others to do so as well.

The next step toward distant healing would be noncontact Therapeutic Touch, as taught by Dolores Krieger and Janet Quinn, both of whom are nursing professors in New York. Krieger and Quinn have taught tens of thousands of nurses highly successful visualization techniques that allow them to focus their healing energies and intentions on their patients in a hospital setting without their hands ever actually touching the sick person's body. Barbara Brennan, founder of her own healing school on Long Island, would also be described as an energy healer. All of these practitioners teach their students to feel, visualize, and experience various forms of vital, psychic, or healing energy, whether in a contact or a noncontact mode.

In the realm of noncontact healing, there are two modes of operation: psychic healing and spiritual healing. A psychic healer accomplishes healing of a distant person through an act of will. The spiritual healer, on the other hand, promotes healing through a surrendered connection to a higher power. Patricia Sun has been a well-known healer since the 1970s. I once asked Patricia about this distinction at a dinner party. She said, "I have to admit it: I do it all by myself." In a recent Internet interview, Patricia Sun spoke of how her healing skills first emerged:

> I had gone to the University of California, had a degree in conservation and one in psychology, and I was doing

family counseling for about two years. During that time, in the early seventies, I "opened." I started reading people. I started intuitively knowing. One of the first things I learned was about left brain and right brain. The left side was really the receptive side. And, when I was doing counseling, right from the very beginning, I would notice a difference in the way I thought when I was successfully helping people and when I was overly concerned with being right and figuring out what was wrong and even relying on training. I was less effective. In fact, it polarized people. When I moved to my soft mind and just had love for the person and I opened myself to whatever could be helpful to them, different things happened. I would have flashes, I would see something. And I remember one time this woman burst into tears, and what I was picking up, though I did not know how, was something that had happened to her, the trauma that had caused the problems we'd been talking about. So I was working with people, and in two or three sessions people were having tremendous insights. I realized that this was not regular therapy, and that perhaps I didn't really want to be a psychologist in the model that psychology used.[20]

Olga and Ambrose Worrall were among the most well known spiritual healers in the United States in the mid-twentieth century. Ambrose was an engineer by day, but he and his wife held weekly healing services at their New Life Clinic in a Methodist church in Baltimore, Maryland. Sometimes more than three hundred people came to them for healing each week. During their morning healing sessions in the church, they administered laying-on-of-hands healing, which Olga said was an important part of a neophyte spiritual healer's development.

The Worralls, however, were probably best known for the distant healings they did in the evenings from their home. Every night at 9:00 P.M., the Worralls observed a five-minute period of silence for absent healing. They encouraged people in need of healing to "tune in" and join these prayer times. Thousands of people who believed they were helped by the Worralls' distant-healing prayers wrote them letters of thanks; these letters have been saved at the Worrall Institute in Springfield, Missouri. Here is how Olga described her letting-go, or "surrendered," approach to becoming a channel for spiritual healing:

> Energy from the universal field of energy becomes available to the healer through the act of tuning his personal energy field to a harmonious relationship with the universal field of energy.... He acts in this way as a conductor between the universal field of energy and the patient.[21]

DISTANT HEALING IN THE LAB

In his 1993 book *Healing Research,* psychiatrist Daniel Benor examined over fifty controlled studies from around the world. He reviewed psychic, mental, and spiritual healing experiments performed on a variety of living organisms: enzymes, cell cultures, bacteria, yeasts, plants, animals, and humans. More than half the studies demonstrated significant healing. His 2001 book, *Spiritual Healing,* describes more than 120 scientific studies.[22]

A Study on Prayer and AIDS

A landmark study by Fred Sicher, psychiatrist Elisabeth Targ, and others was published in the December 1998 issue of the *Western Journal of Medicine,* describing healing research carried out at California Pacific Medical Center (CPMC).[23] This research details and describes the positive therapeutic effects of distant healing, or healing intentionality, on men with advanced AIDS.

In this mainstream medical journal, the researchers defined

nonlocal, or distant, healing as "a conscious dedicated act of mentation intended to benefit another person's physical and/or emotional well-being at a distance," adding that it has been found in some form in nearly every culture in history. Their research hypothesized that an intensive ten-week distant-healing intervention by experienced healers located around the U.S. would benefit the medical outcomes for a population of advanced AIDS patients in the San Francisco Bay Area.

The researchers performed two separate, randomized, double-blind studies: a pilot study involving twenty male subjects paired by number of AIDS-defining illnesses, and a replication study of forty men carefully matched into pairs by age, T-cell count, and number of AIDS-defining illnesses. The participants' conditions were assessed by psychometric testing and blood testing at their enrollment, after the distant healing intervention, and again six months later, when physicians reviewed their medical charts.

In the pilot study, four of the ten control subjects died, while all of the subjects in the treatment group survived. But this result was possibly confounded by unequal age distributions in the two groups.

In the replication study, men with AIDS were again recruited from the San Francisco Bay Area. This time, they were paired more thoroughly, as described above. They were told that they had a fifty-fifty chance of being in the treatment group or the control group.

Forty distant healers from all parts of the country took part in the study. Each of them had more than five years of experience with their particular form of healing. They were from Christian, Jewish, Buddhist, Native American, and shamanic traditions, as well as from secular "bioenergetic" schools. Each patient in the healing group was treated by a total of ten different healers on a rotating schedule. Healers were asked to work on their assigned subject for approximately one hour per day for six consecutive days, with instructions to "direct an intention of health and well-being" to the subject. None of the forty subjects in the study ever met the healers, nor did they or the experimenters know into which group anyone had been randomly assigned.

After five weeks, at the midpoint of the study, neither group of subjects was able to guess whether they were the healing group. By the end of the study, however, there were many fewer opportunistic illnesses in the healing group, allowing the group's members to identify themselves as such — with significant odds against chance. Since all subjects were being treated with Triple-Drug Therapy, there were no deaths in either group. The healing group experienced significantly better medical and quality-of-life outcomes (odds of 100 to 1) on many quantitative measures, including fewer outpatient doctor visits (185 vs. 260); fewer days of hospitalization (10 vs. 68); less severe illnesses acquired during the study, as measured by illness severity scores (16 vs. 43); and significantly less emotional distress. In her summary, Elisabeth Targ concluded, "Decreased hospital visits, fewer new severe diseases, and greatly improved subjective health supports the hypothesis of positive therapeutic effects of distant healing."

The editor of the journal introduced the paper thus: "The paper published below is meant to advance science and debate. It has been reviewed, revised, and re-reviewed by nationally known experts in biostatistics and complementary medicine. We have chosen to publish this provocative paper to stimulate other studies of distant healing, and other complementary practices and agents. It is time for more light, less dark, less heat [fewer arguments]."

Other Clinical Demonstrations of Distant Healing

Two other balanced, double-blind studies of distant healing have been published in prestigious medical journals. In 1988, physician Randolph Byrd published, in the *Southern Medical Journal*, a successful double-blind demonstration of distant healing. The study involved 393 cardiac patients at San Francisco General Hospital.[24] In 1999, cardiologist William Harris of the University of Missouri in Kansas City published a similar successful study with 990 heart patients.[25]

The outcomes of all three clinical experiments departed significantly from chance expectation. The work of Sicher and Targ, however, required fewer than one-tenth the number of patients involved in the other studies to achieve this significance. One possible explanation for this greater effect size $[Z/(N)^{1/2}]$ is the fact that Sicher and Targ worked with healers who each had more than five years of healing experience, whereas the others worked with well-intentioned but much less experienced people.[26]

A detailed analysis of twenty-three clinical studies of intercessory prayer and distant healing has recently been published by John Astin et al. in the *Annals of Internal Medicine*.[27] An examination of sixteen studies that they found to have adequate double-blind designs showed a relatively large effect size of 0.4, with an overall significance of 1 in 10,000 for 2,139 patients. In addition, two excellent analyses of the mechanisms for distant intentionality and distant healing studies have been published in *Alternative Therapies in Health and Medicine* by Marilyn Schlitz and William Braud,[28] and by Elisabeth Targ.[29]

why bother

with esp?

DISCOVERING THAT YOU ARE
THE LOVE YOU SEEK

If you haven't discovered who you truly are, your assumed competence is just a wall of sand against the oncoming tide.

—Tarthang Tulku

Remote viewing is not necessarily a spiritual path, but it can lead us there, giving us the mind-quieting tools and experience to follow some of the well-trodden paths that have been described for millennia. More important, our experience with remote viewing shows without a doubt that we can learn to expand our unconditioned awareness through all of space and time — to directly explore the timeless existence described by the mystics. Allowing your awareness to expand into this feeling of spaciousness is one of the great rewards of this practice; you open the gates, and out flows who you are.

It is increasingly recognized that our physical and mental health require that we take personal initiative to control our chattering minds. The quiet mind has the opportunity to experience what Jesus called "the peace that passeth understanding." As I described earlier, between the inflow of remote viewing and the outflow of spiritual healing, we can experience the overwhelming peace and oceanic connection that is available to each of us in the present moment. In the present, there is neither perception nor intention — just pure awareness. Our ability to share this experience of freedom, love, and spaciousness is what gives meaning to our lives. With our present technology of television, video games, e-mail, and computers, however, we run the risk of never having another quiet moment. This represents the greatest loss we could possibly experience.

Carl Sagan was a great astronomer and a celebrated teacher, but he found the idea of God to be incomprehensible.[1] Why couldn't this brilliant man find God? From my observations and reading, I think it was because he could never be quiet. Beyond that, as an astronomer he thought God was to be found on the outside, rather than on the inside. Powerful telescopes will not help us in our search for love, peace, or God.

In fact, much suffering is caused by looking on the outside for what is actually on the inside. I believe that the spiritual practice that works for the twenty-first century is, first of all, to resolutely desire freedom from the conditioned awareness of our story and our past, and then to find a way to be still. The path I am describing asserts that the existence of God is a testable hypothesis. The American mystic Joel Goldsmith tells us that God is not an entity, but rather, "God may be experienced as an activity in consciousness," like a flow of loving awareness. Many wisdom teachers seem to agree that in order to discover who we really are, we must find a path that allows us to surrender fear, coveting, and craving, then quiet the mind in spite of all the advertising designed to create needs that make us suffer.

TEACHINGS ALONG THE QUIET PATH

On this important subject of stuff and necessities in our lives, my teacher Gangaji writes:

> I invite you to not get anything. You see what a relief it is already? Already there is an opening. I invite you to not remember anything, to not keep anything, to not use any-thing, to not accumulate anything, to not have anything when you walk out the door. How about not having any-thing right now? And if you can truly hear that, then you have heard what I have to teach, because in the moment of not having anything, which is the moment of death, there is a revelation of who you are. But who you are needs noth-ing, and you have the capacity as nothing to realize your-self fully. Not "nothing" as you would think "nothing" to be — something as useless. And not "nothing" as you would hope "nothing" to be — something that would be very useful. You could say, "Well, I have nothing, so now I am free." Not that either.
>
> Then there is conversation that naturally takes place, whether words are involved or not. There is a transmission from mind to mind, from heart to heart, that naturally, effortlessly occurs. That is what we are here for.[2]

Father Thomas Keating, a revered Catholic priest and mystic who teaches centering prayer, says, "God's first language is silence. Everything else is a bad translation."[3]

"Thou art that" is the recurrent theme through the Vedas and the Bhagavad Gita. This is Vedic shorthand for the profound teaching that we already have the whole universe within us, within our awareness. That, of course, includes the love we are looking for outside ourselves.[4] The contemporary musician and teacher Kenny Werner writes in his inspiring book, *Effortless Mastery*, "It is said that one drop of ecstasy from the Self, the God inside us, renders all other pursuits insignificant. At that point, the seeker has found everything he has sought."[5]

My personal goal has been, for many years, to turn a rocket scientist into a human being. I have believed that a human being could experience more meaning in life and more peace of mind than a rocket scientist.

I have been a professional scientist for more than forty years, in the fields of both laser physics and parapsychology research. Although I was trained as a physicist, over the past twenty-five years I have somehow coauthored five books — all of which have "mind" in their titles. While physics attempts to reveal the mysteries of the material universe, it has curiously little to say about mind or consciousness. Over the years, I have become passionate about understanding the nature of consciousness and how it allows our awareness to transcend space and time — for, indeed, it does.

For more than a decade, I toiled with thousands of my fellow engineers in the aerospace slave pits of a large defense contractor in Palo Alto, California. I was well paid, and I had created an exciting research program to put lasers on commercial airplanes, enabling them to detect and avoid dangerous wind hazards. We had even designed a system to do this kind of laser-based remote sensing from outer space, allowing me to think of myself as a "rocket scientist." The bad news is that my inner space was filled with fear, resentment, anger, and desperation.

I've managed to move myself from a wage-slave mentality of fear and desperation to a life that is focused increasingly on gratitude and love. My purpose in writing this book is to be helpful — to help others find peace as I have now found. It may be hard to imagine, but the significant love available to us transcends girl-friends, boyfriends, romance, or sex. The love that I'm talking about is the love that exists at our core. If you are vigilant, no one can ever separate you from that love.

I learned about this love through the grace of the spiritual teacher Gangaji, a brilliant, beautiful, compassionate American woman and mystic. She teaches self-inquiry in the tradition of *advaita* and the Indian saint Ramana Maharshi.[6] It is through her loving transmission that I made the transition, eight years ago, from hard-edged scientist to mashed potato — a more serene, happy human being. After a weeklong retreat with Gangaji in the mountains of Colorado, I returned to my desk at Lockheed Missiles & Space, and told them, with the greatest of ease, that I was leaving. It's not that there was anything wrong with my job, but it had become an absurd way for me to spend my life. I launched myself on a different path to spaciousness that didn't require a missile.

The mind, when it is quiet and open, has the opportunity to be overwhelmed by love. Buddhists call this "undifferentiated awareness." Just as love is the core teaching in Christianity, experiencing our unbounded and undifferentiated awareness *(sunyata)*[7] is one of the principle teachings in Buddhism. This is the teaching of empty, empty, happy, happy — whereas, in Silicon Valley, where I live, "full, full, happy, happy" is the usual goal. Initially, the latter seems like a good idea, but over the millennia it has invariably been found to fail, for the hungry ghost within the ego never has enough. The hungry ghost is the one with the big belly, tiny mouth, and skinny neck; it can never eat enough to be full.

I am not encouraging you to believe in any particular doctrine, since I know from my own experience that many people, especially scientists, would rather suffer fear, anxiety, and depression than believe anything that might be thought silly or doctrinaire. Silliness, for a scientist, is a fate worse than death. I am,

however, telling you that life is much, much more enjoyable from
where I stand now.

A Course in Miracles

The main stepping-stones on my path to truth and freedom
are provided by the teachings of *A Course in Miracles*[8] and by
Dzogchen Buddhism. The approach of *A Course in Miracles* to a
meaningful life has been followed by millions of people since the
book first appeared in 1975. The *Course* came as a gift, unsolicited,
in the consciousness of another scientist, Dr. Helen Schucman, a
clinical psychology professor at Columbia-Presbyterian Hospital in
New York. As you might imagine, the last thing in the world that
a Jewish psychology professor was looking for was the voice of Jesus
in her head, whispering spiritual teachings and commanding her to
write them down. Nevertheless, with the encouragement of her
colleague Bill Thetford, she did write them down. The words she
received were of such beauty and power that they have inspired and
transformed people's lives all over the world, and they've been translated into a dozen languages.

I met Helen Schucman in 1976, when *A Course in Miracles* was
first published by my dear friend Judy Skutch. Dr. Schucman
was an astute, caustic, humorous woman. Even after seven years of
transcribing the *Course* from the dictation of an inner voice, she
was sure she didn't understand it all. I had an unopened first edi-
tion of *A Course in Miracles* on my shelf for over fifteen years
before Jane Katra recommended that I actually read it, which I did
with the help of a study group. The book came off the shelf when
it had finally become obvious that my life wasn't working or bringing me the happiness that I felt was possible. I was miserable in my
job, I had become quite ill, and my marriage was falling apart. It
is often such suffering that brings people to a spiritual search.

The message of the *Course* is conveyed succinctly in Gerry

Jampolsky's charming little book, *Love Is Letting Go of Fear.*9 This is a wonderful self-help book aimed at reducing suffering and fostering self-improvement.

The language of *A Course in Miracles* is beautiful, poetic, and sometimes difficult to understand. Familiar words are frequently used in unfamiliar ways — an effective way to stop the mind's chatter and force one to give up judgment and analysis. The goal of the *Course* is self-realization — a more lofty aspiration than just cleaning house. It explains that our separation from each other is an illusion, just as Jesus taught us to "Love your neighbor as yourself." This precept about separation is precisely the same as is taught in the Vedas, the oldest spiritual books of India. The highest Vedic teaching is the nondual, nonjudgmental Advaita Vedanta. It teaches that, although our bodies appear to be separate from one another, our consciousness is not.

Nonduality refers to the idea that most things are neither true nor not true, but rather the result of our projection onto them. The Buddhists teach that every time you make a distinction, you make an error and cause suffering. Nonduality is an invitation to give up all ideas of separation and judgment (but not necessarily discernment). It is important to realize the inherent duality of our prevailing religious monotheism. The idea of an omnipotent, vengeful deity out there necessarily separates one from the direct experience of God within. This approach is obviously dualistic, and a cause of unnecessary suffering. The idea of a loving God within is nondualistic and leads to peace.

As I described in Chapter 1, physicists in laboratories around the world have recently demonstrated the truth of this non-local connection, which physicist David Bohm called "quantum interconnectedness." The idea of nonseparation is powerfully described in Ken Wilber's book *One Taste,* in which he writes, "The body, mind, and soul are not mutually exclusive. The desires

of the flesh, the ideas of the mind, and luminosities of the soul —
all are perfect expressions of the radiant spirit that alone inhabits
the universe."[10] Wilber says that this reflects the important truth
that, whereas we can open our hand only to its fullest extent, there
is no limit to the extent to which we can open our mind.

In addition to having some strong common roots with
Vedanta, it seems clear to me that *A Course in Miracles* has several
significant commonalities with the very nonreligious philosophy
of existentialism, as taught by Jean-Paul Sartre. As in Sartre's
thinking, the *Course* teaches that we ourselves give all the meaning
there is to everything we experience, offering us absolute freedom,
together with absolute responsibility. Sartre taught that freedom is
man's inescapable ontological (relating to existence) condition.
Sartre's depressing "meaninglessness" comes from the fact that,
although he knew we have full control and responsibility for
everything we do, he apparently did not realize that we have the
same control over our thoughts — from which we derive our
meaning. Similarly, the *Course* says, "What I see reflects a process
in my mind, which starts with my idea of what I want."

Along this same line, the Buddhists would say that impermanence and pain cannot be avoided, but suffering is optional;
suffering comes from attachment to our "stories" and our fear, and
from confusing our bodies with our true selves — the essence of
conditioned awareness. Similarly, the *Course* says that bodies are
only for learning and communicating; although we reside as bodies, that is not who we are. As we become increasingly attached to
our things, our bodies, and the bodies of other people, we open
ourselves to endless suffering. This is because even when we win
"the prize" — whoever or whatever it is — happiness comes and
goes in a microsecond, and we return to our previous state of
unfulfillment and desire. Happiness is never accomplished; it only
ensues as a process.

I have learned that a miracle is a shift in perception, not some kind of supernatural occurrence. Changes in our perception alter how we experience events in our lives. *A Course in Miracles* says that miracles occur naturally, and that as we change our point of view we alter our perception of time and space. The nonlocal connections that physicists talk about were experienced and described in detail 2,400 years ago and recorded as the Sutras of Patanjali, as discussed in Chapter 1. These early teachings, which are remarkably consistent with modern physics, are reiterated in *A Course in Miracles*, as well as in other esoteric traditions.

Huxley's perennial philosophy, as described in Chapter 1, maintains that we have a dual nature — both local and nonlocal, both material and nonmaterial — and that the nonmaterial part is eternal, surviving bodily death.[11] It also teaches that the essential purpose and meaning of our lives is to become one with this universal nonlocal consciousness, which is always available to us. That is, the purpose of life is to become one with God and, through compassion, help others to do the same.

In his introductory Dzogchen text *Kindly Bent to Ease Us*, Longchenpa discusses the critical importance of pursuing meaning in our lives, and gives us this warning:

> If a person is to set out on his quest for life's meaning, he must already have a conviction that life holds meaning, and have a vision of its meaningfulness. If, in this lifetime, you do not make good use of your existence, you will in the hereafter *not even hear the words* "happy life-form."[12]

Jewish psychiatrist Viktor Frankl spent three years in a German concentration camp, but nonetheless was able to see that each day the choice must be made either to open our hearts or to perish. In his inspiring book, *Man's Search for Meaning*, he tells us that even under the torturous conditions of the death camps, people had the spiritual freedom to choose the attitudes they wished to embody. He writes: "It is this spiritual freedom — which cannot be taken away — that makes life meaningful and purposeful."[13]

Frankl also believed that life's meaning comes from experiencing something greater than oneself. This "something" — this experience of unitive consciousness, unbounded by bodies or distance — is often called God or limitless love. It is an experience, not a belief. Novelist Henry Miller tells us, "The goal of life is not to possess power, but to radiate it."[14]

The Course has further helped me realize that we find purpose and meaning by surrendering our ego or separateness to the love that is at our core, and helping others to do the same. This is the "meaning of life" that Monty Python didn't tell us about in the popular film by that name. This teaching of helpfulness is a constant objective throughout almost all spiritual teachings: Buddhist, Hindu, Jewish, and Christian. A Course in Miracles says of our purpose:

I am here only to be truly helpful...
I do not have to worry about what to say, or what to do,
Because He who sent me will direct me. (Text: 24)

The use of the term "He" when referring to God has presented great difficulties to scientists, feminists, existentialists, and many others who have given some thought to life's meaning. For many people, this anthropomorphic God is the greatest stumbling block to a spiritual life. If God is merely a man, then the rational mind is driven to look for meaning in another place. However, if God is the experience of oneness and the oceanic connection that the mystic feels when meditating and is overwhelmed by love, then we might consider exploring the path. The big discovery is that you already have within yourself the love you think you are looking for. You are that love.

This is not romantic love, but rather the transcendent love of God, the experience of which is called *ananda,* or spiritual bliss, in the Hindu scriptures. This is love without an object. Surrendering to this love is more like being in warm, loving syrup than desiring something from another person. This surrender opens a free-flowing conduit to the love of God. We can reach this experience through meditation, contemplative prayer, or the assistance of a gifted teacher. Many of us also find this experience through reading *A Course in Miracles* and doing the lessons in the *Course in Miracles Workbook.*

Such teaching can help you break open your heart, allowing you to see your friends and the world through the eyes of love. With such an experience, neither you nor the world will be the same again. Many teachers in the Advaita tradition can and do help a student to have such a heart-bursting experience if the student meets the teacher with a heart that is ready to open. I have seen some people caught completely off guard and have their lives instantly changed forever, merely by the teacher's presence or through a meditative insight. When Christians teach that God is love, this is not only a metaphor; it can be seen as a pure mystic or Gnostic Christian expression of what is available. I believe that we are all looking for such an experience. Sometimes a lack of connection in a person's life makes him or her unhappy, sick, or angry. When we meet a person suffering this disconnection from his or her loving self, the *Course* would have us remember that every encounter we have "is either an expression of love or a call for love." In the language of the *Course,* there is only love or fear.

I am a scientist and a fairly unreconstructed Aries, so patience is not one of my strong points. When I go shopping or engage in other everyday frustrations, it is often hard for me to remember that half the people in the world have IQs under 100, or that they may be brilliant but do not speak English. But I see that although their experience in the world may be different from mine, their search for the experience of God — of love — is the same. Every encounter can be seen as a holy encounter with a fellow seeker, giving either an expression of love or a call for love. Again, we cannot find love outside ourselves. Instead, we must look inward for the barriers of fear that we have erected against love's appearance, which is the timeless and often subliminal experience of God. A person may feel it but be unaware of what that feeling is.

The Sufi poet Jelaluddin Rumi reminds us that we see our own beauty in others. In all the mystical paths, the *experience* of God is celebrated, rather than the belief in God or the ritual around such a belief. Rumi has written:

All day I think about it, then at night I say it.
Were did I come from, and what am I supposed to be
    doing?
I have no idea.
My soul is from elsewhere, I'm sure of that,
And I intend to end up there.[15]

FORGIVENESS IS THE KEY

Carrying a grudge is like carrying a red-hot rock or giving the person who hurt you a lifetime of free rent in your mind. Why would you want to do that? In some families, grievances and resentment are held for years, even decades. We forgive people who we imagine have harmed us because, for our own mental health, we want to lay down the burden of the past rather than carry it into the present.

I know from experience that these feelings can corrode the soul. I was falsely maligned by a coworker twenty years ago, and I lost my job as a result. I was hurt deeply by this self-centered action of a person who I thought was my friend. Ten years ago, when I had a possible recurrence of cancer, I met Jane Katra, a spiritual healer and immune-system coach who became my teaching partner for a decade. Jane told me that if I wanted to become healthy, one of the many things I would have to do was rid my mind of past grievances and resentments because they limit the free flow of love through my awareness and my body.

I learned that old resentments — whether perceptions or misperceptions — are stumbling blocks to mental and physical health because they keep the mind tethered to the past. Our minds must be still, relaxed, and open in the present moment to perceive the presence of love, and thereby facilitate healing.

As a result of Jane's suggestions, I worked on forgiveness. I called the man who had wronged me and told him I was sorry that we had ever had such a disagreement. He replied that he, too, regretted it and was not proud of many things he had done. At lunch the next week, he gave me several photographic records of research we had done together in the past, greatly facilitating the publication of a book I was then working on.

It appears that forgiveness is an essential step on the road to peace. It is not forgetting, but forgiving and letting go that heals all separations. For me, forgiving was the first step toward my own peace and healing.

The great Hindu mystic Shankara taught that the most important thing for us to learn is the discernment of reality from illusion. We then discover that most of what we thought we were experiencing was, in fact, illusion.[16] Furthermore, the Buddhists teach that there is virtually no objective reality to our judgments, so they usually lead to errors, and often to suffering. In our personal lives, our judgment of others always separates us from the loving connection with God.

In my most steadfast Silicon Valley days, it seemed that a day without judgment was like a day without sunshine. My judgments of others and my attachment to material possessions and cherished outcomes resulted in fear, desperation, and riding my motorcycle through the foothills without a helmet. In the past, through my attachment to control and judgment, I would defend myself and puff up my ego with many forms of nothingness, but it never worked. Since my goal has become to reside in love, I no longer want to pollute my environmental mind-stream with judgment and gossip. I have found that teachings as diverse as the Advaita and the Kabbalah instruct us to transcend our limiting ideas of who we think we are — separate egos and entities — if we are to have freedom.

I have a great friend who is an intelligent and discerning businessman. He has learned to make his highly successful way in the world through astute use of his judgment and critical skills, even though as a result he's overcome with negativity. For many years, I was amused by hearing the outrageous verbal pictures he painted' of his life in the financial district of San Francisco. These pictures were populated with brilliantly drawn and hugely flawed people. We would laugh together over how silly people can be — especially highly placed people. I no longer find this kind of conversation amusing, however; it just makes me tired. Incredibly, I have lost all interest in participating in these judgments, and I even find them painful. I now realize that this kind of cynicism and judgment is actually hazardous to my health.

Choosing Again

I have learned to check my premises and choose again to find peace. In the 1950s, the work of philosopher and novelist Ayn Rand taught me that every person must be a philosopher and continually "check his premises" for contradictions. Harboring contradictions makes us crazy and makes our lives incoherent, preventing us from reaching our life's objectives. *A Course in Miracles* teaches:

I must have decided wrongly, because I am not at peace. I made the decision myself, but I can decide otherwise.[17]

The *Course* encourages us to "choose again." I believe in heaven and hell, but they are both in my head. When I am joyful and peaceful, I am in heaven. When I am angry and fearful, I am in hell. And in every moment I get to choose again. The poet John Milton put it perfectly: "A mind is its own place, and in itself can make a heaven of hell, a hell of heaven."[18]

The longing for God that our heart experiences is, in fact, a reflection of our actual connection with God. We can awaken each morning in gratitude for another day of limitless possibilities. For me, resting in God reflects the Christian idea of "prayer without ceasing." It doesn't mean going about all day pleading and mumbling prayers. It means going about with an awareness of our connection to God and to each other. It is an awareness of gratitude for each breath and each green leaf. I have even learned to be grateful for red traffic lights; they give me an uninterrupted minute or two, in which there is no other thing that I must do except experience gratitude for my entire situation — the beautiful surroundings, the canopy of trees, the golden light of a California afternoon. Or I can choose to pound the handlebars of my motorcycle and curse the slowness of the light in changing. It is entirely my choice.

In regard to remote viewing and its relationship to spirituality, the *Course* raises the question in its "Manual for Teachers," "Are 'psychic' powers desirable?" It answers by saying:

There are, of course no "unnatural" powers, and it is obviously merely an appeal to magic to make up a power that does not exist. It is equally obvious, however, that each individual has many abilities of which he is unaware. As his awareness increases, he may well develop abilities which appear quite startling to him. Yet nothing he can do can compare even in the slightest with the glorious surprise of remembering who he is.

The *Course* is continually teaching that, if you don't like what you are experiencing, "choose again." Similarly, Dzogchen tells us (annoyingly) that *samsara* (the world of everyday suffering) and *nirvana* (the world of peace and bliss) are simply two perceptions of the same reality. Again, the teaching is that these are just ideas held in our minds and projected onto our experience of the world. But the prison can be escaped. Freedom is at hand by becoming aware of this process.

Namkhai Norbu is a contemporary Dzogchen master living in Italy. He has written many books; one of the most accessible and inspiring is *The Mirror: Advice on the Presence of Awareness.* He is trying, through direct transmission, to propel the reader out of conditioned awareness and into timeless existence. Freedom and spaciousness are the objectives. He writes:

> Dzogchen doesn't ask you to change your religion, philosophy, or ideology, nor to become something other than what you are. It only asks you to observe yourself, and to discover the "cage" you have built with your conditioning and limits. And it teaches you how to get out of the cage, without creating another one, in order to become a free, autonomous person.[19]

The message of *The Mirror,* as in all Dzogchen teachings, is one of crystal clarity and "pristine awareness": It is critically important for each of us to remember, and remain aware, that we are the mirror, and not all the chaotic things that are reflected in it. Norbu specifically says, "You are the mirror, not the reflection." He discusses the extent to which the conditioned mind is the source of suffering. In order to continually reside in the flow of loving awareness, we must block the flow of the river of our discontent. Following an extended river analogy, he tells us that the river must be blocked at its source, not after it has become a raging torrent. Similarly, to get rid of a giant weed in our garden, it won't do to prune the leaves and shoots; it must be pulled out by the roots. And, of course, the source and root of our suffering is in our mind and our judgments. The necessary pruning cannot be accomplished by "virtuous acts." Wearing a hair shirt to torment the body, starving oneself, or denying one's natural sexuality will not bring freedom. One must overthrow the conditioned mind in order to "conquer the kingdom and achieve freedom."

Longchenpa's advice in "The Jewel Ship" is as powerful today as when it was written in the twelfth century.[20] He describes the "five passions of conditioned existence." These define the all-too-familiar walls of the cage that Norbu is helping us to flee — or to awaken to the fact that we are not actually in a cage at all. Longchenpa doesn't want us to fixate on these hindrances to freedom; he suggests that we just notice them and let them go. The five passions to be released are:

1.   Lust: not to be confused with love, nor allowed to run your life (lust is always about something external to be gotten);

2.   Anger: always in service to the small self or ego ("They're not doing it my way!")

3.   Arrogance: puffed up with infinite nothingness; the tragic confusion of oneself with one's story;

4.   Jealousy: ignoring the fact that we already have within us limitless love and everything else we could possibly want;

5.   Stupidity: knowing the truth and choosing differently.

Like the seven "deadly sins," each of us will have our own personal favorite among these five passions.

In writing of the passions from which our cages are built, I can't help thinking of our beloved Marilyn Monroe. Everyone loved Marilyn Monroe; she had money, beauty, fame, security, means of expression, and great recognition. Since these are things that we all seek, and she had them in abundance, why did she keep trying to kill herself — and eventually succeed?

At this point in the chapter, we all know the answer: She had no idea who she was. She created "Marilyn Monroe" as a supreme comedic accomplishment. Lee Strasberg of the Actor's Studio and playwright Arthur Miller both thought she was one of the greatest actresses of the century. Her tragedy is that she believed that her posters, her made-up persona, and her business card represented who she was, rather than just being her story.

My teacher Gangaji has written an exquisite little book called *Freedom and Resolve,* describing the path of self-inquiry and the life-and-death issue of discovering who we are.[21] In a chapter called "The Story of 'Me,'" she inescapably presents the importance of recognizing our story for what it is, and then — in spite of what our ego says — surrendering it. She writes:

> The first challenge is to recognize that you are telling a story. Then the challenge is in having the willingness to die, and in that, the willingness to be nothing at all. Then, this that we have called Self or Truth or God is revealed to be that very same no-thing at all. You recognize yourself as that no-thing.

I interpret this using the following example: Engineers at Lockheed often work there for a lifetime — thirty or more years. When they retire, they often live a shockingly short time. By my calculation, they die significantly sooner than actuarially predicted, by odds of twenty to one. This is scary for those of us who worked there. I suspect that the reason for their premature death has something to do with the fact that business cards (or "story" cards) from there define one as a "Lockheed (or Boeing) Engineer." When one retires after a lifetime of service, one suddenly becomes nothing. This is the serious penalty one can pay for believing one's "story."

All people have fundamental requirements for peace of mind and happiness: security (food and shelter), expression of one's inner feelings, recognition as a person, and a feeling of belonging to something. Viktor Frankl teaches that, in order for our lives to have meaning, we must also have compassion and generosity. Referring to "belonging" or community, Rabbi Hillel said, "If I am not for myself, who will be for me? If I am only for myself, I am nothing."

TIMELESS EXISTENCE

As we learn to open our hearts, we have the opportunity to reside in love, compassion, joy, and equanimity — what the Dzogchen masters call "spontaneous equalness." Heart-opening leads to the experience of freedom and the "truth of the heart." Dzogchen is profoundly in favor of heart-opening and experiencing this transcendent flow of loving awareness, but it also recognizes that one has a head, a brain, a mind, and, above all, limitless awareness. It is this awareness (which is who you are) that will not be peaceful and satisfied until it has achieved its potential, satisfied its inner need and drive, and expanded into the spaciousness of timeless existence.

Other forms of Buddhism are heart-centered and emphasize, first, the teachings of the "Four Noble Truths" and the "Eightfold Way" to escape suffering and achieve liberation or freedom, as taught by Buddha in the Deer Park. And, secondarily, the Bodhisattva path comprises emptiness and compassion for the removal of suffering for all sentient beings. Dzogchen offers a third path where we have the opportunity to experience the truth of the heart in addition to the ultimate freedom, the truth of the universe. I am finally learning to travel that blessed path each night at bedtime, and each morning as I awaken, in gratitude.

I am convinced that timeless awareness and spaciousness is our goal. If that is too big a step, however, there is always gratitude, which is everyone's salvation. If we can awaken in the morning and, instead of feeling fear or resentment, give thanks to God — or the organizing principle of the universe that gives us our good health and our good minds — we are well on the way to peace and freedom. We are actually giving thanks for grace — the unsolicited gifts we have all been given. I have found that while I am in a state of gratitude, it is impossible for me to be unhappy.

While we cannot always control the events around us, we do have power over how we experience those events. At any moment, we can individually and collectively affect the course of our lives by choosing to direct our attention to the aspect of ourselves that is aware and, through the practice of self-inquiry, to awareness itself. We can ask, "Who is aware?" and then, "Who wants to know?" The choice of where we put our attention is ultimately our most powerful freedom. Our choice of attitude and focus affects not only our own perceptions and experiences, but also the experiences and behaviors of others.

It is my pleasure to end this chapter, and this book, with a quote from the greatest of Dzogchen masters, Longchenpa. He reminds us that we already have everything we could possibly want. In his powerful transmission known as "The Jewel Ship," he gives us a meditation called "Making Your Free Behavior the Path." After that, nothing more can be said — except to offer you the Buddhist prayer of *metta,* or loving kindness.

From Longchenpa:

> Listen great being [that's you]: do not create duality from
> the unique state.
> Happiness and misery are one in pure and total presence.
> Buddhas and beings are one in the nature of mind.
> Appearances and beings, the environment and its inhabi-
> tants, are one in reality.
> Even the duality of truth and falsehood are the same reality.
> Do not latch onto happiness; do not eliminate misery.
> Thereby everything is accomplished.
> Attachment to pleasure brings misery.
> Total clarity, being nonconceptual, is self-refreshing pristine
> awareness.

And from my own heart:

> May you be in peace.
> May your heart remain open.
> May you be healed from all separation.
> May you be a source of healing for all beings.
> May you awaken to the light of your true nature.
> May you never feel separate from the source of loving
> kindness.
> May you be happy.

elisabeth's
story

My daughter Elisabeth was a lifelong explorer and seeker after truth. Her luminosity and visionary thinking were evident to all who knew her, and were apparent in her television interviews.[1] As a child, Elisabeth was encouraged to be polite, intelligent, and psychic. She was able to describe, for example, what was inside her birthday presents before she opened them.

At the memorial service for her at California Pacific Medical Center, where she worked until her passing, the research director described her as "probably the smartest person I ever met." Her widely praised research in distant healing at that hospital showed that prayerful healers across the United States could affect the health and well-being of seriously ill AIDS patients in San Francisco. As I mentioned in Chapter 6, she demonstrated, in a study that was published in the *Western Journal of Medicine,* that patients receiving healing prayers felt more mentally positive about themselves, had fewer opportunistic illnesses and significantly fewer trips to the hospital, and spent fewer days in the hospital than the control group for whom no prayers were said.[2] This result occurred in spite of the fact that neither the patients nor the doctors knew which patients were receiving the prayers — a "double-blind" experiment. This gave meaningful, real-life evidence for our nonlocal, mind-to-mind connections, and encouraged the National Institutes of Health (NIH) to support similar research at other laboratories.

Since childhood, Elisabeth participated in many ESP studies with me. As a nine-year-old, she was an early participant in an ESP teaching-machine experiment that showed that one can learn what it feels like to successfully use one's psychic abilities. The machine would randomly select one of its four possible electronic states, and the user would then press one of the four buttons on the front of the machine to indicate her choice of what the machine had selected. The correct one of four colored lights would then be illuminated. A score of six out of twenty-four was expected by chance. Encouragement messages were: "A Good Beginning" for six correct answers out of twenty-five; "ESP Ability Present" for eight; "Outstanding" for ten; and "Psychic, Medium, Oracle!" for twelve. Some people could learn to increase their score by practice, even though the machine was making its choices randomly. Elisabeth was one of the most successful from the outset, often scoring in the highest category.

In 1971, I decided to take my ESP teaching machine to the general public. I designed a stand-up, coin-operated version, and had it manufactured by a young engineer named Nolan Bushnell, who two years later started the two-billion-dollar Atari Corporation to make his own electronic games. Figure 10 shows nine-year-old Elisabeth with the ESP game in a Palo Alto Round Table pizza parlor. The *San Francisco Chronicle* ran a story on us, and captioned this photo "ESP in a Pizza Parlor." The three installations in Palo Alto were very successful. I couldn't get national distribution for the machine, however; I was told that the distributors in Chicago "didn't know what an ESP was."

Figure 10. Elisabeth Targ operating the first commercial ESP testing machine, 1971. Reprinted by permission of the *San Francisco Chronicle*.

The following year, I had an opportunity to demonstrate this entertaining machine to Werner von Braun and James Fletcher, then the director of NASA. Both men scored well on their practice trials. Von Braun then told us stories about his famously psychic grandmother back in the old country, who always knew in advance when something important was going to happen. That encounter at a NASA conference on Speculative Technology eventually led to a NASA contract at Stanford Research Institute (SRI) to help astronauts develop their intuitive psychic contact with their spacecraft.[3] I believe it is always an experience with a "psychic grandmother" that convinces government bureaucrats to give money for ESP research!

In 1983, Elisabeth — then twenty-one years old and a medical student at Stanford — accompanied me on a trip to Russia, where I had been invited to talk to the U.S.S.R. Academy of Sciences on the remote-viewing research I was doing at SRI. I asked her to come with me because she was already a competent Russian translator. Her grandmother, Regina, attended medical school in Russia in the 1930s, and her mother, Joan, was born there at that time. After graduating from Stanford University, Elisabeth had spent a year meeting the requirements for her translator's certificate, wisely deciding that she didn't want to start medical school until she was at least twenty.

Elisabeth had seen me show slides and describe my SRI remote-viewing research to scientific groups many times. On this particular occasion, we were seated in tall red-velvet chairs on the stage of the U.S.S.R. Academy of Sciences in Moscow. I was to give my slide show, and a Russian translation would follow each of my sentences.

There were three or four hundred scientists in the opulent, gilded auditorium as we were just beginning the laborious "he-said, she-said," translation process. As the light from the huge crystal chandelier dimmed, I felt a tugging on my sleeve. Elisabeth had come to the podium to respectfully suggest to me that if she gave my talk in Russian from the start, it would go much more smoothly. So, trusting my daughter, I introduced her and sat down to watch the show. She proceeded to describe the decade of research material with which she was quite familiar. I could hear the whispering and the teacups rattling as people tried to figure out how this young woman knew the physics, psychology, and statistics necessary to present a 90-minute data-filled talk, without notes and in unaccented Russian.

Elisabeth was a sensation, charming our hosts wherever we traveled and lectured, from Moscow to Leningrad, from Alma Ata in the far east to the Russian Science City in Siberia. As we arrived at each venue, our hosts already knew our preferences and set places for us with cognac, while everyone else at the table drank vodka. We felt like the talk of Russia.

Figure 11. Elisabeth Targ (left) and Russell Targ at an artist's studio in Tbilisi, southern Russia, on their 1983 trip. Photo by Hella Hammid.

Nothing in Russia starts without some sort of drink. At the Radio Technical Institute in Moscow, where our first SRI remote-viewing papers were translated into Russian, there was a daily coffee break at 10:30 A.M. The lovely little tea wagon came tinkling down the hall to visit each office, and its host would inquire whether we wanted vodka, cognac, or tea for breakfast. The scientists there often described their work situation to us by saying, "They pretend to pay us, and we pretend to work." That was at the height of the Cold War; it is likely that everything is less elegant today. After that time, Elisabeth visited Russia frequently on her own, both as a student and as a researcher. She spoke with some of the legendary Russian spiritual healers, including our dear friend Djuna Davitashvili, with whom we had done remote-viewing experiments for the Academy of Science.

Beginning with our earliest father-daughter ESP experiments, I would sit in a chair and visualize an object, then invite Elisabeth to sit in the same chair and try to experience the object I had imagined. This kind of "thought form" investigation would have pleased Charles Leadbeater, Annie Besant, and the other nineteenth-century theosophical researchers. We had much success.

With that sort of early training, it is no wonder that Elisabeth was often described as an "out of the box" scientist even before the phrase became popular. She took on investigations of some of the most challenging medical conditions known to science and society. Her research interests spanned an uncommon range of issues, including schizophrenia and how it could be misdiagnosed when, in fact, a patient was having a spiritual awakening. The research also dealt with psychoneuroimmunology, learned helplessness in mental health, the health benefits of meditation and contemplative prayer, and the impact of spiritually transforming experiences on the field of psychiatry itself.

Figure 12. Elisabeth Targ: 1961–2002. This photo is from the cover of the California Pacific Medical Center newsletter announcing Elisabeth's successful AIDS research.

Elisabeth's fatal illness was a glioblastoma. Remarkably, this is the particular kind of brain tumor that was the subject of her most recent research in distant healing. She said she chose it for the study because it was a particularly "gnarly" or incurable disease — the same reason she felt it was important to choose AIDS for her first study.

Elisabeth peacefully moved beyond this plane of illusion on July 18, 2002. In her passing, Elisabeth is once again a pioneer — the first of her generation to know the truth, while the rest of us are left to speculate and wonder. We all miss her. What a lovely illusion she was.

AUTHOR'S PREFACE

1   Longchenpa, *You Are the Eyes of the World* (Ithaca, NY: Snow Lion Publications, 2000). Also see the wonderful transmission by Longchen Rabjam, *The Precious Treasury of The Way of Abiding* (Junction City, CA: Padma Publishing, 2002).

2   W. Y. Evans-Wentz, *The Tibetan Book of the Dead* (New York: Oxford University Press, 1960).

3   *A Course in Miracles: Workbook for Students* (Huntington Station, NY: Foundation for Inner Peace, 1975).

INTRODUCTION: THE UNKNOWABLE END OF SCIENCE

1   Erwin Schrödinger, *What Is Life* (Cambridge: Cambridge University Press, 1945).

2   Michio Kaku, "Techniques of Discovery" (lecture presented at The Prophets Conference, New York City, May 18–20, 2001).

3   Steven Weinberg, "The Future of Science and the Universe," *New York Review of Books*, November 15, 2001.

4   Corey S. Powell, *God in the Equation* (New York: The Free Press, 2002).

5   Harold Puthoff and Russell Targ, "A Perceptual Channel for Information Transfer over Kilometer Distances: Historical Perspective and Recent Research," Proc. IEEE, vol. 64, no. 3, March 1976, Brenda Dunne and Robert Jahn, "Information and Uncertainty in Remote Perception Research," *Journal of Scientific Exploration*, vol. 17, no. 2, Summer 2003, pp. 207–242.

CHAPTER 1: OUR LIMITLESS MIND

1   Alan H. Batten, "A Most Rare Vision: Eddington's Thinking on the Relation between Science and Religion," *Journal of Scientific Exploration*, vol. 9, no. 2, Summer 1995, pp. 231–34.

2   For an in-depth discussion of this phenomenon, see Guy Lyon Playfair, *Twin Telepathy: The Psychic Connection* (London: Vega, 2003).

3   A. Einstein, B. Podolsky, and N. Rosen, "Can a Quantum Mechanical Description of Physical Reality be Considered Complete?" *Physical Review* 47, 1935, pp. 777–780.

4   J. S. Bell, "On the Einstein, Podolsky, Rosen Paradox," *Physics* 1, 1964, pp. 195–200.

5   S. Freedman, and J. Clauser, "Experimental Test of Local Hidden Variable Theories," *Physical Review Letters*, vol. 28, 1972, 934–941.

6   Henry Stapp, in R. Nadeau and M. Kafatos, *The Nonlocal Universe: The New Physics and Matters of the Mind* (London: Oxford University Press, 1999).

7   J. W. Dunne, *An Experiment with Time* (1927; reprint, Charlottesville, VA: Hampton Roads, 2001).

8   Brenda Dunne and Robert Jahn, "Information and Uncertainty in Remote Perception Research," *Journal of Scientific Exploration*, vol. 17, no. 2, 2003, pp. 207–242.

9   David Bohm and B. Hiley, *The Undivided Universe* (London: Routledge, 1993), pp. 382–386.

10   Eugene P. Wigner, "The Extension of the Area of Science," in Robert G. Jahn, *The Role of Consciousness in the Physical World*, AAAS Symposium 57 (Boulder, CO: Westview Press, 1981).

11   Elizabeth Rauscher and Russell Targ, "The Speed of Thought: Investigation of a Complex Space-Time Metric to Describe Psychic Phenomena," *Journal of Scientific Exploration*, vol. 15, no. 3, Fall 2001.

12   Upton Sinclair, *Mental Radio* (Charlottesville, VA: Hampton Roads, 2001).

13   C. W. Misner and John Wheeler, "Gravitation, Electromagnetism, Unquantized Charge, and Mass as Properties of Curved Empty Space," *Annals of Physics* 2, December 1957, pp. 525–603.

14   Brian Josephson, "Biological Utilization of Quantum Nonlocality," *Foundations of Physics*, vol. 21, 1991, pp. 197–207.

15   Aldous Huxley, *The Perennial Philosophy* (New York: Harper and Row, 1945).

16   Erwin Schrödinger, *Mind and Matter* (Cambridge: Cambridge University Press, 1958).

17   Elaine Pagels, *Beyond Belief: The Secret Gospel of Thomas* (New York: Random House, 2003).

18   I mention this here because the revered teacher Ram Dass admonishes all who have had their first heart-opening experiences through the use of psychoactive drugs to tell the truth, and not to pretend that the opening occurred through years of meditation.

19   Lawrence Kushner, *The River of Light* (Woodstock, VT: Jewish Lights Publishing, 1981, 1990).

20   Lex Hixon, *Mother of the Buddhas: Meditation on the Prajnaparamita Sutra* (Wheaton, IL: Quest Books, 1993).

21   Helen Palmer, *The Enneagram: Understanding Yourself and the Others in Your Life* (San Francisco: Harper San Francisco, 1991).

22   Eli Jackson-Bear, *The Enneagram of Liberation: From Fixation to Freedom* (Stinson Beach, CA: The Leela Foundation, 2002).

23   J. L. Garfield, *The Fundamental Wisdom of the Middle Way: Nagarjuna's Mulamadhyamakakarika* (London: Oxford University Press, 1995).

24   Swami Prabhavananda and Christopher Isherwood, trans., *How to Know God* (Hollywood, CA: Vedanta Press, 1983).

25 Andrew Harvey, *The Essential Mystics: The Soul's Journey into Truth* (San Francisco: Harper San Francisco, 1996).

CHAPTER 2: ON A CLEAR DAY WE CAN SEE FOREVER

1   In fact, like twins raised apart, Hal and I were both only children, were born in Chicago, and went to work for the Sperry Gyroscope Company as our first job. In the late 1950s we were working on the development of high-power microwave tubes at different Sperry locations before we switched to laser research, moved to California, and began to pursue psi research, after which we finally met in 1972.

2   There are now more than a dozen ex-army men and women teaching remote viewing in the U.S., and more than 119,000 "remote viewing" Websites to be found on the Google search engine. Remote viewing is a natural ability and a relatively easy one to learn, so it's likely that a number of the established remote viewing schools can show you how to do it. None of them publish any information about double-blind tests, so it's impossible to determine whether viewers can actually learn and succeed at remote viewing or if they simply learn what the process entails. I do not believe there is presently any evidence that there is a benefit to paying thousands of dollars to attend such remote viewing classes, but I could be wrong. I would suggest, instead, that you continue reading this book, or Ingo Swann's wonderful book, *Natural ESP* (New York: Bantam Books, 1987).

    The public is often confused about the claims of remote viewing teachers. There is Controlled Remote Viewing (CRV®), Extended Remote Viewing (ERV®), Technical Remote Viewing (TRV®), and probably others of which I'm unaware. Joe McMoneagle, who was one of the first and by far the most successful of the army remote viewers, has written an excellent book, *Remote Viewing Secrets* (Charlottesville, VA: Hampton Roads, 2000), in which he unscrambles these acronyms. He also describes a very clear and sensible approach to learning remote viewing, based on his more than twenty years of experience.

3   Russell Targ and Jane Katra, *Miracles of Mind: Exploring Nonlocal Consciousness and Spiritual Healing* (Novato, CA: New World Library, 1998).

4   Russell Targ and Hal Puthoff, "Information Transfer under Conditions of Sensory Shielding," *Nature* 251, 1974, pp. 602–607.

5   The Intuition Network promotes business-related and other applications of psi work.

6   Patricia Hearst, *Every Secret Thing* (New York: Doubleday & Company, 1982).

7   Ingo Swann, *Natural ESP* (New York: Bantam Books, 1987).

8   Daryl Bem and Charles Honorton, "Does Psi Exist? Replicable Evidence for an Anomalous Process of Information Transfer," *Psychological Bulletin*, January 1994.

9   Marilyn Schlitz and Charles Honorton, "Ganzfeld Psi Performance within an Artistically Gifted Population." *Journal ASPR*, vol. 86, 1992, pp. 83–98.

10   In card-guessing, the viewer knows that the target will be one of four or five possible shapes. That knowledge constitutes mental noise and prevents the viewer from seeing mental pictures on a blank screen.

11   C. W. Leadbeater, *Occult Chemistry* (London: Theosophical Society, 1898).

12   Russell Targ and Jane Katra, *Miracles of Mind: Exploring Nonlocal Consciousness and Spiritual Healing* (Novato, CA: New World Library, 1998).

13   Russell Targ, E. May, and Hal Puthoff, "Direct Perception of Remote Geographic Locations," in *Mind At Large: Proceedings of the IEEE Symposia on Extrasensory Perception* (Charlottesville, VA: Hampton Roads, 2002).

14   James Spottiswoode, "Geomagnetic Fluctuations and Free Response Anomalous Cognition: A New Understanding," *Journal of Parapsychology* 61, March 1997.

15   A sidereal day is about four minutes shorter than a solar day. You can determine your present sidereal time at various Internet sites, including www.jgiesen.de/astro/astroJS/siderealClock/ (accessed October 2003). For additional sites, search at www.google.com for "local sidereal time."

16   H. W. Parke, *The Delphic Oracle* (London: Basil Blackwell, 1966).

17   René Warcollier, *Mind-to-Mind* (Charlottesville, VA: Hampton Roads, 2002).

CHAPTER 3: FOR YOUR VIEWING PLEASURE

1   Robert Monroe describes this exciting continuum — from remote viewing to "sex on the astral plane" — in his pioneering book, *Journeys Out of the Body* (New York: Broadway Books, 1973). This now-classic book is wonderful reading. Another excellent book for those with a courageous and adventurous spirit is *Psychic Sexuality*, by Ingo Swann (Rapid City, SD: Ingo Swann Books, 1999).

2   Russell Targ and Jane Katra, "Remote Viewing in a Group Setting," *Journal of Scientific Exploration*, vol. 14, no. 1, 2000, pp. 107–114.

3   John Reynolds, *Self-Liberation through Seeing with Naked Awareness* (Ithaca, NY: Snow Lion Publications, 2000).

4   Padmasambhava, in John Reynolds, *Self-Liberation through Seeing with Naked Awareness* (Ithaca, NY: Snow Lion Publications, 2000).

5   Dixon, N. F., *Subliminal Perception: The Nature of a Controversy* (London: McGraw-Hill, 1971).

6   Sheila Ostrander and Lynn Schroeder, *Psychic Discoveries Behind the Iron Curtain* (New York: Prentice-Hall, 1970).

7   Richard Bach, *Jonathan Livingston Seagull* (New York: Scribner Book Company, 1970).

8   Joe McMoneagle, *Remote Viewing Secrets* (Charlottesville, VA: Hampton Roads, 2000).

CHAPTER 4: PRECOGNITION

1   Bertrand Russell, *Mysticism and Logic and Other Essays* (London: Longmans, Green and Co., 1925).

2   Robert Monroe, *Journeys Out of the Body* (New York: Broadway Books, 1973).

More information about things to do while out of your body, and how to get there, can be obtained from the Monroe Institute in Faber, Virginia.

3 Erwin Schrödinger, in Michael Nielsen, "Rules for a Complex Quantum World," *Scientific American*, November 2002.

4 Charles Honorton and Diane Ferrari, "Future-Telling: A Meta-Analysis of Forced-Choice Precognition Experiments," *Journal of Parapsychology*, vol. 53, December 1989, pp. 281–209.

5 William Braud, "Wellness Implications of Retroactive Intentional Influence: Exploring an Outrageous Hypothesis," *Alternative Therapies in Health and Medicine*, vol. 6, no. 1, 2000, pp. 37–48.

6 Dean Radin, *The Conscious Universe* (San Francisco: Harper San Francisco, 1997).

7 William Braud, *Distant Mental Influence* (Charlottesville, VA: Hampton Roads, 2003).

8 Zoltán Vassy, "Method for Measuring the Probability of 1 Bit Extrasensory Information Transfer Between Living Organisms," *Journal of Parapsychology*, vol. 42, 1978, pp. 158–160.

9 Helmut Schmidt, "PK Effect on Pre-Recorded Targets," *Journal of the American Society for Psychical Research*, July 1976.

10 Helmut Schmidt, "Random Generators and Living Systems as Targets in Retro-PK Experiments," *Journal of the American Society for Psychical Research*, vol. 91, no. 1, 1997, pp. 1–14.

11 William Braud, "Wellness Implications of Retroactive Intentional Influence: Exploring an Outrageous Hypothesis," *Alternative Therapies in Health and Medicine*, vol. 6, no. 1, 2000, pp. 37–48.

12 Erik Larson, "Did Psychic Powers Give Firm a Killing in the Silver Market?" *Wall Street Journal*, Oct. 22, 1984.

13 Russell Targ, Jane Katra, Dean Brown, and Wendy Wiegand, "Viewing the Future: A Pilot Study with an Error-Detecting Protocol," *Journal of Scientific Exploration*, vol. 9, no. 3, 1995, pp. 367–380.

14 David Bohm, *The Undivided Universe* (New York: Routledge, 1993).

15 Norman Friedman, *Bridging Science and Spirit: Common Elements of David Bohm's Physics, the Perennial Philosophy, and Seth* (St. Louis, MO: Living Lake Books, 1994).

16 Gertrude Schmeidler, "An Experiment in Precognitive Clairvoyance, Part 1: The Main Results" and "Part 2: The Reliability of the Scores," *Journal of Parapsychology*, vol. 28, 1964, pp. 1–27.

17 Elisabeth Targ, Russell Targ, and Oliver Lichtarg, "Realtime Clairvoyance: A Study of Remote Viewing without Feedback," *Journal of the American Society for Psychical Research*, vol. 79, October 1985, pp. 494–500.

18 Brenda Dunne and Robert Jahn, "Information and Uncertainty in Remote Perception Research," *Journal of Scientific Exploration*, vol. 17, no. 2, 2003, pp. 207–242.

19 Montague Ullman and Stanley Krippner with Alan Vaughan, *Dream Telepathy* (Charlottesville, Virginia: Hampton Roads, 2003).

20   Russell Targ and Harold Puthoff, *Mind Reach: Scientists Look at Psychic Abilities* (New York: Delacorte, 1977), p. 50.

21   Harold Puthoff and Russell Targ "A Perceptual Channel for Information Transfer over Kilometer Distances: Historical Perspective and Recent Research," *Proceedings of the IEEE*, vol. 64, no. 3, March 1976, pp. 329–354.

22   Olivier Costa de Beauregard, in J. T. Fraser, *The Voices of Time* (New York: George Braziller, 1966).

23   *Ibid.*

24   J. W. Dunne, *An Experiment with Time* (Charlottesville, VA: Hampton Roads, 2001).

25   B. J. Dunne, R. G. Jahn, and R. D. Nelson, "Precognitive Remote Perception," *Princeton Engineering Anomalies Research Laboratory* (Report), August 1983.

26   Elisabeth Targ and Russell Targ, "Accuracy of Paranormal Perception as a Function of Varying Target Probabilities," *Journal of Parapsychology*, vol. 50, March 1986, pp. 17–27.

27   F. W. H. Myers, *Human Personality and Its Survival of Bodily Death* (Charlottesville, VA: Hampton Roads, 2001).

28   Harold Francis Saltmarsh, *The Future and Beyond: Paranormal Foreknowledge and Evidence of Personal Survival from Cross Correspondences* (Charlottesville, VA: Hampton Roads, 2004).

29   Daniel J. Benor, *Spiritual Healing: Scientific Validation of a Healing Revolution* (Southfield, MI: Vision Publications, 2001).

CHAPTER 5: INTUITIVE MEDICAL DIAGNOSIS

1   Arthur Hastings, *Tongues of Man and Angels* (Austin, TX: Holt, Rinehart & Winston, 1991).

2   Gina Cerminara, *Many Mansions: The Edgar Cayce Story on Reincarnation* (New York: Signet Books, 1967).

3   The best evaluation of the medical readings can be found at the Website of the Meridian Institute: http://www.meridianinstitute.com.

4   Judith Orloff, *Second Sight* (New York: Warner Books, 1997).

5   Judith Orloff, *Intuitive Healing* (New York: Three Rivers Press, 2000).

6   John Woodroffe, *The Serpent Power* (Madras, India: Ganesh & Co., 1928, 1964).

7   Mona Lisa Schultz, *Awakening Intuition* (New York: Three Rivers Press, 1998).

8   Anthony Goodman, *Understanding the Human Body: Anatomy and Physiology: 32 Lectures* (Chantillly, VT: The Teaching Company, 2001).

9   Shafrica Karagulla, *Breakthrough to Creativity* (Marina del Rey, CA: Devorss & Co., 1967).

10   This was a warm-up experiment for my going to Cambridge, where I was to talk with physicists who were investigating the direct perception of very large magnetic fields through the production of what are called visual phosphenes — probably caused by electric currents in the eye. While at

Cambridge, I also worked with some electric fish at the Cavindish Aquarium. These blind African fish, called gymnarcus, could detect and respond to very small permanent magnetic fields. I could call them to the front of their large glass tank by moving a small magnet (or, it seemed to me, by an act of will, as William Braud found in his research a decade later — but that's another story).

11 Karagulla, *Breakthrough to Creativity.*
12 Barbara Brennan, *Hands of Light* (New York: Bantam Books, 1987); also, Barbara Brennan, *Light Emerging* (New York: Bantam Books, 1993).
13 C. Norman Shealy and Caroline Myss, *The Creation of Health* (Walpole, NH: Stillpoint Publishing, 1988).
14 Marianne Williamson, in Russell Targ and Jane Katra, *The Heart of the Mind: How to Experience God without Belief* (Novato, CA: New World Library, 1999), from the foreword.

CHAPTER 6: DISTANT HEALING

1 Tom Harpur, *The Uncommon Touch: An Investigation of Spiritual Healing* (Toronto: McClelland & Stewart, Inc., 1994), pp. 38–73.
2 Holy Bible, John, 14:12.
3 Energy healers feel, visualize, or otherwise experience and direct healing energy toward their patients' bodies; this may or may not involve physical contact. Psychic and spiritual healing are both noncontact modes. Psychic healers direct their will toward the healing of a distant patient, while spiritual healers surrender themselves to a higher power to accomplish distant healing.
4 Larry Dossey, *Meaning and Medicine* (New York: Bantam Books, 1991).
5 Milan Ryzl, "A Model of Parapsychological Communication," *Journal of Parapsychology,* 1966, pp. 18–30.
6 L. L. Vasiliev, *Experiments in Mental Suggestion* (Charlottesville, VA: Hampton Roads, 2002).
7 Henry Stapp, "Harnessing Science and Religion: Implications of the New Scientific Conception of Human Beings," *Research News and Opportunities in Science and Religion* vol. 1, no. 6, p. 8 (February, 2001).
8 Douglas Dean, "Plethysmograph Recordings as ESP Responses," *International Journal of Europsychiatry,* vol. 2, 1966, pp. 439–446.
9 A plethysmograph registers variations in the size of an organ or limb resulting from changes in the amount of blood present in or passing through it.
10 William Braud and Marilyn Schlitz, "Consciousness Interactions with Remote Biological Systems: Anomalous Intentionality Effects," *Subtle Energies,* vol. 2, 1993, pp. 1–47; William Braud, "On The Use of Living Target Systems in Distant Mental Influence Research," in L. Coly, ed., *Psi Research Methodology: A Re-examination* (New York: Parapsychology Foundation, 1991).

11   All of William Braud's work that is referenced here can also be found in his
     new book, *Distant Mental Influence* (Charlottesville, VA: Hampton Roads,
     2003).

12   William Braud, "Direct Mental Influence on the Rate of Hemolysis of
     Human Red Blood Cells," *The Journal of the American Society for Psychical
     Research,* January 1990, pp. 1–24.

13   William Braud, *Distant Mental Influence* (Charlottesville, VA: Hampton
     Roads, 2003).

14   William Braud and Marilyn Schlitz, "Psychokinetic Influence on Electro-
     Dermal Activity," *Journal of Parapsychology,* vol. 47, 1983, pp. 95–119;
     William Braud, D. Shafer, and S. Andrews, "Reactions to an Unseen Gaze
     (Remote Attention): A Review, with New Data on Autonomic Staring
     Detection," *Journal of Parapsychology,* vol. 57, no. 4, 1993, pp. 373–390.

15   Marilyn Schlitz and Stephen LaBerge, "Autonomic Detection of Remote
     Observation: Two Conceptual Replications," *Institute of Noetic Sciences,*
     1994 (preprint).

16   Braud, *Distant Mental Influence.*

17   Russell Targ and Harold Puthoff, *Mind Reach: Scientists Look at Psychic
     Abilities* (New York: Delacorte, 1977); Russell Targ and Harold Puthoff,
     "Information Transmission under Conditions of Sensory Shielding,"
     Nature, vol. 252, Oct. 1974, pp. 602–607.

18   Larry Dossey, *Recovering the Soul* (New York: Bantam Books, 1989); Larry
     Dossey, *Healing Words: The Power of Prayer and the Practice of Medicine* (San
     Francisco: Harper San Francisco, 1993); Larry Dossey, *Meaning and Medi-
     cine: A Doctor's Tales of Breakthrough and Healing* (New York: Bantam, 1991).

19   Larry Dossey, *Utne Reader,* September 1995.

20   Patricia Sun, quoted from interview at http://www.phenomenews.com/
     archives/mch01/sun.html (accessed October 2003).

21   Olga Worrall, in Edwina Cerutti, *Olga Worrall: Mystic with the Healing
     Hands* (New York: Harper & Row, 1975).

22   Daniel J. Benor, *Spiritual Healing: Scientific Validation for a Healing Revo-
     lution* (Southfield, Mich.: Vision Publications, 2001).

23   Fred Sicher, Elisabeth Targ, Dan Moore, and Helene Smith, "A Random-
     ized Double-Blind Study of the Effect of Distant Healing in a Population
     with Advanced AIDS," *Western Journal of Medicine,* vol. 169, December
     1998, pp. 356–363.

24   Randolph C. Byrd, "Positive Therapeutic Effects of Intercessory Prayer in a
     Coronary Care Unit Population," *Southern Medical Journal,* vol. 81, no. 7,
     July 1988, pp. 826–829.

25   William S. Harris et al., "A Randomized, Controlled Trial of the Effects of Remote
     Intercessory Prayer on Outcomes in Patients Admitted to the Coronary Care
     Unit," *Archives of Internal Medicine,* vol. 159, October 25, 1999, pp. 2273–2278.

26   The *effect size* measures the efficiency, or strength, of the phenomenon under
     investigation. It is equal to the number of observed standard deviations

from chance, divided by the square root of the number of trials performed in order to achieve that level of significance.

27 John A. Astin, Elaine Harkness, and Edward Ernst, "The Efficacy of 'Distant Healing': A Systematic Review of Randomized Trials," *Annals of Internal Medicine,* vol. 132, no. 11, June 2000, pp. 903–910.

28 Marilyn Schlitz and William Braud, "Distant Intentionality and Healing: Assessing the Evidence," *Alternative Therapies in Health and Medicine,* vol. 3, no. 6, November 1997.

29 Elisabeth Targ, "Evaluating Distant Healing: A Research Review," *Alternative Therapies in Health and Medicine,* vol. 3, no. 6, November 1977.

CHAPTER 7: WHY BOTHER WITH ESP?

1 Carl Sagan, *The Demon-Haunted Universe: Science as a Candle in the Dark* (New York: Ballantine, 1997).

2 Internet message, 9/1/03.

. 3 Thomas Keating, *Intimacy with God* (New York: Crossroad Publishing, 1994).

4 The Hindu teaching that *Atman* equals *Brahman* means that our own soul, or center of awareness, is coincident with the entire universe. Erwin Schrödinger, the great physicist who perfected quantum mechanics, refers to this as the greatest principle in all of metaphysics. Erwin Schrödinger, *My View of the World* (Woodbridge, CT: Ox Bow Press, 1983).

5 Kenny Werner, *Effortless Mastery* (New Albany, IN: Jamey Abersold, Inc., 1996).

6 For more information about Gangaji's teachings and programs, please see her Website at www.gangaji.org.

7 *Sunyata* is a Sanskrit word of significance in the Buddhist texts. It pertains to emptiness, impermanence, and spaciousness. It regards the persistent delusion of "inherent existence" as a major obstacle to spiritual development, as well as being the root of many other damaging delusions.

8 *A Course in Miracles* (Huntington Station, NY: Foundation for Inner Peace, 1975).

9 Gerald Jampolsky, *Love Is Letting Go of Fear* (Berkeley, CA: Celestial Arts, 1979).

10 Ken Wilber, *One Taste* (Boston: Shambhala, 1999).

11 The evidence for survival is strongly presented in the cross-correspondence data of F. W. H. Myers (see Chapter 4) and in Ian Stevenson's data from children remembering past lives. Ian Stevenson, *Where Reincarnation and Biology Intersect* (Westport, CT: Praeger, 1997).

12 Longchenpa, *Kindly Bent to Ease Us* (Emeryville, CA: Dharma Publishing, 1975).

13 Viktor Frankl, *Man's Search for Meaning* (New York: Simon & Schuster, 1959).

14 Henry Miller, quoted in Daniel Pinchbeck, *Breaking Open the Head: A*

Psychedelic Journey into the Heart of Contemporary Shamanism (New York: Broadway Books, 2003).

15 Jelaluddin Balkhi Rumi, *The Illuminated Rumi*, trans. by C. Barks with J. Moyne (New York: Broadway Books, 1997).

16 Shankara, *Crest-Jewel of Discrimination*, trans. by Christopher Isherwood (Hollywood, CA: Vedanta Press, 1975).

17 *A Course in Miracles* (Huntington Station, NY: Foundation for Inner Peace, 1975).

18 John Milton, quoted in Pinchbeck, *Breaking Open the Head*.

19 Namkhai Norbu, *The Mirror: Advice on the Presence of Awareness* (Barrytown, NY: Station Hill Openings, 1996).

20 Longchenpa, "The Jewel Ship," in *You Are the Eyes of the World* (Ithaca, NY: Snow Lion Publications, 2000).

21 Gangaji, *Freedom and Resolve: The Living Edge of Surrender* (Novato, CA: The Gangaji Foundation, 1999).

AFTERWORD

1 Such as those by Jeffrey Mishlove, in his *Thinking Allowed* series on Public Television.

2 Fred Sicher, Elisabeth Targ, Dan Moore, and Helene Smith, "A Randomized Double-Blind Study of the Effect of Distant Healing in a Population with Advanced AIDS," *Western Journal of Medicine*, vol. 169, December 1998, pp. 356–363.

3 Russell Targ, Phyllis Cole, and Harold Puthoff, "Development of Techniques to Enhance Man/Machine Communication," SRI Final Report under contract 953653 NAS7–100, 1975; Russell Targ and David Hurt, "Learning Clairvoyance and Precognition with an ESP Teaching Machine," *Parapsychology Review*, July–August 1972.

A Course in Miracles: Workbook for Students. Huntington Station, NY: Foundation for Inner Peace, 1975.

Anand, Margot. *Sexual Ecstasy: The Art of Orgasm.* New York: Jeremy Tarcher/Putnam, 2000.

Astin, John A., Elaine Harkness, and Edward Ernst. "The Efficacy of 'Distant Healing': A Systematic Review of Randomized Trials." *Annals of Internal Medicine* 132 (2000): 903–910.

Barks, Coleman and Michael Green. *The Illuminated Rumi.* New York: Broadway Books, 1997.

Batten, Alan H. "A Most Rare Vision: Eddington's Thinking on the Relation between Science and Religion." *Journal of Scientific Exploration* 9, no. 2 (Summer 1995): 231–34.

Bell, J. S. "On the Einstein, Podolsky, Rosen Paradox." *Physics* 1 (1964): 195–200.

Bem, D., and Honorton, C. "Does Psi Exist? Replicable Evidence for an Anomalous Process of Information Transfer." *Psychological Bulletin,* Jan. 1994.

Benor, Daniel J. *Spiritual Healing: Scientific Validation of a Healing Revolution.* Southfield, MI: Vision Publications, 2001.

Bohm, D. and B. Hiley. *The Undivided Universe.* New York: Rutledge, 1993.

Braden, Gregg. *The Isaiah Effect.* New York: Three Rivers Press, 2000.

Braud, William. "Direct Mental Influence on the Rate of Hemolysis of Human Red Blood Cells." *Journal of Parapsychology* 47 (1983): 95–119.

———. *Distant Mental Influence.* Charlottesville, VA: Hampton Roads, 2003.

———. "On the Use of Living Target Systems in Distant Mental Influence Research." In L. Coly, ed. *Psi Research Methodology: A Re-examination.* New York: Parapsychology Foundation, 1993.

———. "Wellness Implications of Retroactive Intentional Influence: Exploring an Outrageous Hypothesis." *Alternative Therapies in Health and Medicine* 6, no. 1 (2000).

Braud, William and Marilyn Schlitz. "Consciousness Interactions with Remote Biological Systems: Anomalous Intentionality Effects." *Subtle Energies* 2 (1991): 1–47.

———. "Psychokinetic Influence on Electro-Dermal Activity." *Journal of Parapsychology* 47 (1983): 95–119.

Braud, W., D. Shafer, and S. Andrews. "Reactions to an Unseen Gaze (Remote Attention): A Review, with New Data on Autonomic Staring Detection." *Journal of Parapsychology* 57, no. 4 (1993): 373–390.

Brennan, Barbara. *Hands of Light.* New York: Bantam Books, 1987.

———. *Light Emerging.* New York: Bantam Books, 1993.

Byrd, Randolph C. "Positive Therapeutic Effects of Intercessory Prayer in a Coronary Care Unit Population." *Southern Medical Journal* 81, no. 7 (July 1988): 826–829.

Cerminara, Gina. *Many Mansions: The Edgar Cayce Story on Reincarnation.* New York: Signet Books, 1967.

Dean, Douglas, "Plethysmograph Recordings as ESP Responses." *International Journal of of Europsychiatry* 2 (1966): 439–446.

Dixon, N. F. *Subliminal Perception: The Nature of a Controversy.* London: McGraw-Hill, 1971.

Dossey, Larry. *Healing Words: The Power of Prayer and the Practice of Medicine.* San Francisco: Harper San Francisco, 1993.

———. *Meaning and Medicine.* New York: Bantam Books, 1991.

———. *Recovering the Soul.* New York: Bantam Books, 1989.

Dunne, B. J., R. G. Jahn, and R. D. Nelson. "Precognitive Remote Perception." *Princeton Engineering Anomalies Research Laboratory Report* (August 1983).

Dunne, J. W. *An Experiment with Time.* 1927. Reprint, Charlottesville, VA: Hampton Roads, 2002.

Einstein, A., B. Podolsky, and N. Rosen. "Can a Quantum Mechanical Description of Physical Reality Be Considered Complete?" *Physical Review* 47 (1935): 777–780.

Frankl, Viktor. *Man's Search for Meaning.* New York: Simon & Schuster, 1959.

Freedman, S. and J. Clauser. "Experimental Test of Local Hidden Variable Theories." *Physical Review Letters* 28 (1972): 934–941.

Friedman, Norman. *Bridging Science and Spirit: Common Elements of David Bohm's Physics, the Perennial Philosophy, and Seth.* St. Louis, MO: Living Lakes Books, 1994.

Gangaji. *Freedom and Resolve: The Living Edge of Surrender.* Novato, CA: The Gangaji Foundation, 1999.

———. *You Are That! Vol. II.* Novato, CA: The Gangaji Foundation, 1996.

Garfield, J. L. *The Fundamental Wisdom of the Middle Way: Nagarjuna's Mulamadhyamakakarika.* London: Oxford University Press, 1995.

Gerber, Richard, M.D. *Vibrational Medicine.* Santa Fe: Bear & Company, 1988.

Gisin, N., J. Tittel, H. Brendel, and I. Zbinden. "Violation of Bell Inequalities by Photons More Than 10 km Apart." *Phys. Rev. Lett* 81 (1998): 3563–3566.

Goldsmith, Joel. *A Parenthesis in Eternity.* New York: HarperCollins Publishers, 1963.

Harpur, Tom. *The Uncommon Touch: An Investigation of Spiritual Healing.* Toronto: McClelland & Stewart Inc., 1994.

Harris, William S. et al., "A Randomized, Controlled Trial of the Effects of Remote Intercessory Prayer on Outcomes in Patients Admitted to the Coronary Care Unit." *Archives of Internal Medicine* 159 (Oct. 25, 1999): 2273–2278.

Harvey, Andrew. *The Essential Mystics: The Soul's Journey into Truth.* San Francisco: Harper San Francisco, 1996.

Hastings, Arthur. *With the Tongues of Men and Angels.* Fort Worth, TX: Harcourt College Publishers, 1991.

Hearst, Patricia. *Every Secret Thing.* New York: Doubleday & Company, 1982.

Hixon, Lex. *Mother of the Buddhas: Meditation on the Prajnaparamita Sutra.* Wheaton, IL: Quest Books, 1993.

Honorton, Charles and Diane Ferrari, "Future-Telling: A Meta-Analysis of Forced-Choice Precognition Experiments." *Journal of Parapsychology* 53 (December 1989): 281–209.

Huxley, Aldous. *The Perennial Philosophy.* New York: HarperCollins, 1990.

Jampolsky, Gerald. *Love Is Letting Go of Fear.* Berkeley, CA: Celestial Arts, 1979.

Josephson, Brian, "Biological Utilization of Quantum Nonlocality." *Foundations of Physics* 21 (1991): 197–207.

Kaku, Michio. "Techniques of Discovery." The Prophets Conference, New York City, May 2001.

Karagulla, Shafrica. *Breakthrough to Creativity.* Marina del Rey, CA: Devorss & Co., 1967.

Khan, Sufi Inayat. *The Development of Spiritual Healing.* Geneva, Switzerland: Sufi Publishing Co., Ltd., 1961.

Kushner, Lawrence. *The River of Light.* Woodstock, VT: Jewish Lights Publishing, 1981.

Larson, Erik. "Did Psychic Powers Give Firm a Killing in the Silver Market?" *Wall Street Journal,* Oct. 22, 1984.

Leadbeater, C. W. *Occult Chemistry.* London: Theosophical Society, 1898.

Longchen, Rabjam. *The Precious Treasury of the Way of Abiding.* Junction City, CA: Padma Publishing, 2002.

Longchenpa. "The Jewel Ship." *You Are the Eyes of the World.* Ithaca, NY: Snow Lion Publications, 2000.

———. *Kindly Bent to Ease Us.* Emeryville, CA: Dharma Publishing, 1975.

Maharaj, Sri Nisargadatta. *I Am That.* Durham, NC: The Acorn Press, 1997.

McMoneagle, Joe. *Remote Viewing Secrets.* Charlottesville, VA: Hampton Roads, 2000.

Misner, C. W. and Wheeler, J. "Gravitation, Electromagnetism, Unquantized Charge, and Mass as Properties of Curved Empty Space." *Annals of Physics* 2, December 1957, 525–603.

Monroe, Robert A. *Journeys Out of the Body.* New York: Broadway Books, 1973.

Myers, F. W. H. *Human Personality and Its Survival of Bodily Death.* Charlottesville, VA: Hampton Roads Publishing, 2001.

Newberg, Andrew, Eugene D'Aqili, and Vince Rause. *Why God Won't Go Away: Brain Science and the Biology of Belief.* NY: Ballantine Books, 2002.

Norbu, Namkhai. *The Mirror: Advice on the Presence of Awareness.* Barrytown, NY: Station Hill Openings, 1996.

Orloff, Judith. *Intuitive Healing.* New York: Three Rivers Press, 2000.

————. *Second Sight*. New York: Warner Books, 1997.

Ostrander, Sheila and Lynn Schroeder. *Psychic Discoveries behind the Iron Curtain*. New York: Prentice Hall, 1970.

Palmer, Helen. *The Enneagram: Understanding Yourself and the Others In Your Life*. San Francisco: HarperSanFrancisco, 1991.

Parke, H. W. *The Delphic Oracle*. London: Basil Blackwell, 1953.

Playfair, Guy Lyon. *Twin Telepathy: The Psychic Connection*. London: Vega, 2003.

Powell, Corey S. *God in the Equation*. New York: The Free Press, 2002.

Prabhavananda, Swami. *How to Know God*, translated by Christopher Isherwood. Hollywood, CA: Vedanta Press, 1983.

Puthoff, Harold and Russell Targ. "A Perceptual Channel for Information Transfer over Kilometer Distances: Historical Perspective and Recent Research." *Proceedings IEEE* 64, no. 3 (1976): 329–354.

Puthoff, Harold, Russell Targ, and E. C. May. "Experimental Psi Research: Implications for Physics." In R. G. Jahn, *The Role of Consciousness in the Physical World*, AAAS Selected Symposium 57. Boulder, CO: Westview Press, 1981: 37–86.

Radin, Dean. *The Conscious Universe*. San Francisco: Harper San Francisco, 1997.

Rauscher, Elizabeth and Russell Targ. "The Speed of Thought: Investigation of a Complex Space-Time Metric to Describe Psychic Phenomena." *Journal of Scientific Exploration* 15, no. 3 (Fall 2001): 331–354.

Rumi, Jelaluddin Balkhi. *The Illuminated Rumi*, trans. by C. Barks with J. Moyne. New York: Broadway Books, 1995.

Russell, Bertrand. *Mysticism and Logic and Other Essays*. London: Longmans, Green and Co., 1925.

Ryzl, Milan. "A Model of Parapsychological Communication." *Journal of Parapsychology* (1966): 18–30.

Sagan, Carl. *The Demon-Haunted Universe: Science as a Candle in the Dark*. New York: Ballantine, 1997.

Saltmarsh, Harold Francis. *The Future and Beyond: Paranormal Foreknowledge and Evidence of Personal Survival from Cross Correspondences*. Charlottesville, VA: Hampton Roads, 2004.

Schlitz, Marilyn and William Braud. "Distant Intentionality and Healing: Assessing the Evidence." *Alternative Therapies* 3, no. 6 (November 1997).

Schlitz, Marilyn and Charles Honorton. "Ganzfeld Psi Performance within an Artistically Gifted Population." *Journal of the American Society for Psychical Research* 86 (1992): 83–98.

Schlitz, Marilyn and Steven LaBerge. "Autonomic Detection of Remote Observation: Two Conceptual Replications." Sausalito, CA: Institute of Noetic Sciences, 1994.

Schmeidler, Gertrude. "An Experiment in Precognitive Clairvoyance: Part 1, The Main Results" and "Part 2, The Reliability of the Scores." *Journal of Parapsychology* 28 (1964): 1–27.

Schmidt, Helmut. "PK Effect on Pre-Recorded Targets." *Journal of the American Society for Psychical Research*, July 1976.

————. "Random Generators and Living Systems as Targets in Retro-PK Experiments." *Journal of the American Society for Psychical Research* 91, no. 1 (1997): 1–14.

Schrödinger, Erwin. *Mind and Matter.* Cambridge: Cambridge University Press, 1958.

————. *My View of the World.* Woodbridge, CT: Ox Bow Press, 1983.

————. In Michael Nielsen, "Rules for a Complex Quantum World." *Scientific American,* November 2002.

————. *What Is Life.* Cambridge: Cambridge University Press, 1945.

Schultz, Mona Lisa. *Awakening Intuition.* New York: Three Rivers Press, 1998.

Shankara. In Swami Prabhavananda, *Crest-Jewel of Discrimination.* Hollywood, CA: Vedanta Press, 1975.

Shealy, C. Norman and Caroline Myss. *The Creation of Health.* Walpole, NH: Stillpoint Publishing, 1988.

Sicher, Fred, Elisabeth Targ, Dan Moore, and Helene Smith. "A Randomized Double-Blind Study of the Effect of Distant Healing in a Population with Advanced AIDS." *Western Journal of Medicine* 169 (December 1998): 356–363.

Sinclair, Upton. *Mental Radio.* Charlottesville, VA: Hampton Roads Publishing, 2001.

Spotteswoode, James. "Geomagnetic Fluctuations and Free Response Anomalous Cognition: A New Understanding." *Journal of Parapsychology* 61 (March 1997).

Stapp, Henry. "Harnessing Science and Religion: Implications of the New Scientific Conception of Human Beings." *Research News and Opportunities in Science and Religion* 1, no. 6 (February, 2001): 8.

————. In R. Nadeau and M. Kafatos. *The Nonlocal Universe: The New Physics and Matters of the Mind.* London: Oxford University Press, 1999.

Stevenson, Ian. *Where Reincarnation and Biology Intersect.* Westport, CT: Praeger, 1997.

Storm, Lance and Suitbert Ertel. "Does Psi Exist? Comments on Milton and Wiseman's (1999) Meta-Analysis of Ganzfeld Research." *Psychological Bulletin* 127, no. 3 (2001): 424–433.

Swann, Ingo. *Natural ESP.* New York: Bantam Books, 1987.

————. *Psychic Sexuality: The Bio-Psychic "Anatomy" of Sexual Energies.* Rapid City, SD: Ingo Swann Books, 1999.

Targ, Elisabeth. "Evaluating Distant Healing: A Research Review." *Alternative Therapies in Health and Medicine* 3, no. 6 (November 1977).

Targ, Elisabeth, and Russell Targ. "Accuracy of Paranormal Perception as a Function of Varying Target Probabilities." *Journal of Parapsychology* 50 (March 17–27, 1986).

Targ, Elisabeth, Russell Targ, and Oliver Lichtarg. "Realtime Clairvoyance: A Study of Remote Viewing without Feedback." *Journal of the American Society for Psychical Research* 79 (October 1985): 494–500.

Targ, Russell, Phyllis Cole, and Harold Puthoff. "Development of Techniques to Enhance Man/Machine Communication." SRI Final Report under contract 953653 NAS7-100 (1975).

Targ, Russell, and David Hurt. "Learning Clairvoyance and Precognition with an ESP Teaching Machine." *Parapsychology Review* (July-August 1972).

Targ, Russell, and Jane Katra. "Remote Viewing in a Group Setting." *Journal of Scientific Exploration* 14, no. 1 (2000): 107–114.

Targ, Russell, Jane Katra, Dean Brown, and Wendy Wiegand. "Viewing the Future: A Pilot Study with an Error-Detecting Protocol." *Journal of Scientific Exploration* 9, no. 3 (1995): 367–380.

Targ, R., E. May, and H. Puthoff, "Direct Perception of Remote Geographic Locations." *Mind At Large: Proceedings of IEEE Symposia on Extrasensory Perception.* Charlottesville, VA: Hampton Roads, 2002.

Targ, Russell, and Hal Puthoff. "Information Transfer under Conditions of Sensory Shielding." *Nature* 251 (1974): 602–607.

———. *Mind Reach: Scientists Look at Psychic Abilities.* New York: Delacorte, 1977.

Ullman, Montague and Stanley Krippner with Alan Vaughan. *Dream Telepathy.* Charlottesville, VA: Hampton Roads Publishing, 2003.

Vasiliev, L. L. *Experiments in Mental Suggestion.* Charlottesville, VA: Hampton Roads Publishing, 2002.

Vassy, Zoltán. "Method for Measuring the Probability of 1-Bit Extrasensory Information Transfer Between Living Organisms." *Journal of Parapsychology* 42 (1978): 158–160.

Warcollier, René. *Mind-to-Mind.* Charlottesville, VA: Hampton Roads, 2002.

Weinberg, Steven. "The Future of Science and the Universe." *New York Review of Books* (November 15, 2001).

Werner, Kenny. *Effortless Mastery.* New Albany, IN: Jamey Abersold Inc, 1996.

Wilber, Ken. *No Boundary.* Boston: Shambhala, 1979.

———. *One Taste.* Boston: Shambhala, 1999.

Woodroffe, John. *The Serpent Power.* Madras, India: Ganesh & Co, 1928, 1964.

Buddhism
　　Dzogchen teachings, 16, 17, 20,
　　　23–24, 55, 59, 156, 166, 169–70
　　four-valued logic of, 20
　　on judgments, 163
　　on loving awareness, 22
　　on nonduality, 157
　　on separation as an illusion,
　　　xxviii, 14, 19, 157
　　on suffering, 158
　　on undifferentiated awareness
　　　(sunyata), 155, 189n.7
　on wisdom, 21–22
Bushnell, Nolan, 174
Byrd, Randolph, 148–49

C

Calabrese, Prudence, 117
California Pacific Medical Center
　(CPMC), 146–48
Campbell, Joseph, 78
card-guessing, 41, 184n.10
Carr, Wayne, 117
"A Case of ESP" (NOVA), 90–91
causality, 78–79, 80, 84–85, 89
Cayce, Edgar, 32, 107–8, 109
Cayce, Hugh Lynn, 127
cerebral functioning, 47
Cerminara, Gina, 107
chakras, 109–10, 118
children, 115
choosing again, 164–69
Christianity, on local community of
　spirit, 15
Christian Science, 18
CIA, 32, 36, 66
clairvoyance, 39, 69–70
　See also remote viewing
Clauser, John, 6
collective unconscious, 18
Committee for the Scientific Investi-
　gation of Claims of the Paranor-
　mal (CSICOP), 35

community of spirit, 14–19, 92
compassion, 19
complex Minkowski space, 8–10
conditioned awareness, 22–23, 55, 158
conditioned existence, 167–68
consciousness
　　Hindus on, 101
　　individual vs. universal, 14–15
　　interconnectedness via, xxv
　　local vs. quantum, xix
　　nonlocal universe accessed by,
　　　9–12, 91
　　as omni-dimensional, xx
　　and quantum mechanics, 8
　　unity of, 8, 14
conservation of energy, law of, 12–13
Controlled Remote Viewing
　(CRV®), 183n.2
Copernicus, Nicolas, xxv
A Course in Miracles, xiii, 23, 156–62,
　164–66
Cox, Bart, 96
CPMC (California Pacific Medical
　Center), 146–48
Craig, Mary, 11
Creation of Health (Shealy and Myss),
　122–23
cross-correspondence cases, 102
CSICOP (Committee for the Scien-
　tific Investigation of Claims of the
　Paranormal), 35

D

Dalai Lama, 20
Darwin, Charles, xxv
Dass, Ram, 182n.16
Davitashvili, Djuna, 42, 178
the dead, communication by, 102–3
Dean, Douglas, 132–33
de Beauregard, Olivier Costa, 97–98
DeFreeze, Donald ("Cinque"), 30–32
Delphi Associates, 90–91
determinism, 97–98

intuition, 29, 112
See also medical diagnosis, intuitive
Intuition Network, 28, 183n.5
investments, psychic forecasting of, 34, 34 (fig.), 89–91

J

Jackson-Bear, Eli, 19
Jahn, Robert, 95, 99
Jampolsky, Gerry, 156–57
jealousy, 167
Jesus
as a healer, 125–26
on loving "your neighbor as yourself," 157
on "the peace that passeth understanding," xiii, 4, 152
The Jewel Ship (Longchenpa), 167–68, 170–71
Josephson, Brian, 13
Judaism, 15, 18
judgments, 163–64
Jung, Carl, 18

K

Kabbalah, 164
Kaku, Michio, xxvi
Kant, Immanuel, 7
Karagulla, Shafrica, 120
Katra, Jane, 33, 44, 50, 58, 81–83, 121, 140–41, 163
Keating, Thomas, 153
Kelvin, William Thomson, Lord, xxvi
Kornfield, Jack, 110
Krieger, Dolores, 119, 144
Krippner, Stanley, 95–96
kundalini meditation, 109
Kunz, Dora, 119–20
Kushner, Lawrence, 18

L

LaBerge, Stephen, 137
laws of nature, xvi
laying on of hands, 144, 145
Leadbeater, C. W., 41
Leningrad Institute for Brain Research, 129
life, purpose of, 14, 159–60
location, remote viewing for, 29–32
logic, two-valued vs. four-valued, 19–23
Longchenpa
Dzogchen (great perfection) teachings of, xii, 22–23, 159
The Jewel Ship, 167–68, 170–71
love, 154–55, 160–62
lust, 167

M

magnets/magnetic fields, 119, 186–87n.10
Maharshi, Ramana, 155
McMoneagle, Joe, 27, 45, 55–56, 69–70, 183n.2
MDMA (Ecstasy), 15–16
Mead, Margaret, 16–17, 133
meaninglessness, 158
medical diagnosis, intuitive, 105–23
and the body's energy systems, 108–12
by Cayce, 107–8
data, 119–21
developing your abilities, 114–16
distance from the patient, 106
feeling stage, 115
gathering additional information, 116
mechanism of, 12
medical intuitives, 112–14
overview, xxix
vs. remote viewing, 106, 119
right-brain/left-brain approaches, 116–17

Russell Targ is a physicist and author. He was a pioneer in the development of the laser, and the cofounder of the Stanford Research Institute's investigation into psychic abilities. His scientific work in this new area, called "remote viewing," has been published worldwide. He is the coauthor of five other books dealing with the investigation of psychic abilities. In 1997, Targ retired from his position as a senior staff scientist at Lockheed Missiles & Space Company, where he developed airborne laser systems to detect air turbulence. He now teaches remote viewing, and is publishing special editions of classic books is psychical research. His Website is http://www.espresearch.com.

NEW WORLD LIBRARY is dedicated to publishing books and other media that inspire and challenge us to improve the quality of our lives and the world.

We are a socially and environmentally aware company. We recognize that we have an ethical responsibility to our readers, our authors, our staff members, and our planet.

We serve our readers by creating the finest publications possible on personal growth, creativity, spirituality, wellness, and other areas of emerging importance. We serve our authors by working with them to produce and promote quality books that reach a wide audience. We serve New World Library employees with generous benefits, significant profit sharing, and constant encouragement to pursue their most expansive dreams.

Whenever possible, we print our books with soy-based ink on 100 percent postconsumer-waste recycled paper. We power our Northern California office with solar energy, and we respectfully acknowledge that it is located on the ancestral lands of the Coast Miwok Indians. We also contribute to nonprofit organizations working to make the world a better place for us all.

Our products are available wherever books are sold.

customerservice@NewWorldLibrary.com
Phone: 415-884-2100 or 800-972-6657
Orders: Ext. 110
Fax: 415-884-2199
NewWorldLibrary.com

Scan below to access our newsletter
and learn more about our books and authors.